THE LAWS *of* HAPPINESS

LOVE, WISDOM,

SELF-REFLECTION *and* PROGRESS

RYUHO OKAWA

IRH PRESS

BOOKS
IRH PRESS
New York

ISBN 13: 978-1-942125-70-9
ISBN 10: 1-942125-70-4

Printed in Canada

First Edition

Cover Design: Whitney Cookman

Contents

PREFACE 13

CHAPTER ONE

HOW NOT TO BE UNHAPPY
Overcoming Your Fate

CHAPTER TWO

ONE STEP UP IN YOUR WORK CAPABILITY

Four Ways to Become More Capable

CHAPTER FOUR

INTRODUCTION TO HAPPY SCIENCE

The Mindsets to Happiness for All People

CHAPTER FIVE

BELIEVING THE AGE OF THE SUN WILL COME

The Future Society Led by *The Laws of the Sun*

This book is a compilation of the lectures as listed on page 232.

PREFACE

Since the Laws Series began with the first book, *The Laws of the Sun*, followed by the second book, *The Golden Laws*, I have progressed through this series and written the seventh book, *The Laws of Great Enlightenment*. Now I have reached this eighth book, *The Laws of Happiness*.

I've given a variety of teachings up to this point. But for this book, I've returned to Happy Science's starting point to write about, "What is happiness?"

However I string my words together, the power of my light won't be fulfilling its original mission if the words fail to guide people to the shore of happiness. So, to write this book, I used the simplest possible words—words that people newly encountering the Truths will understand.

Chapter one is titled "How Not to Be Unhappy," and in this chapter I dig up the lonely and worried feelings that everyone has. I teach an unexpected perspective: "In actuality, it's your ways of thinking themselves that are making you unhappy. It's not that it's impossible to become happy. You are seeking to be unhappy without realizing that you are doing so." At first, you might be surprised to hear this, and you may wonder, "Is it at all possible for me to be thinking that inside myself?" But, in truth, it's important to resolve not to be unhappy before you try to become happy.

Chapter two is entitled "One Step Up in Your Work Capability." In this chapter, I picked up what I felt to be the most essential and basic of the many teachings I've given on work capability and management philosophy. These days, many people are working day and night whether at their companies or other places of work. This is why I felt that modern teachings on happiness wouldn't be complete without teachings on improving your work capability.

These are not grandiose teachings on accomplishing great feats of work. What I set down in this chapter came from the perspective of helping you improve your present work capability or working methods by one step. You could think of it as a highly simplified approach. In Happy Science's *shojas* (our large temples), we hold deeper management seminars, but for beginners, I believe that this simple approach will help save even more people.

Chapters three and four bring together my lectures on the principles of happiness, which could be called the modern Fourfold Path. These are the central Laws of my present incarnation. Each of these two chapters explains the four principles of love, wisdom, self-reflection, and progress in a different way. Comparing these two chapters as you read them will help you grasp what I am truly trying to say.

At Happy Science, we essentially teach people to practice the principles of happiness based on exploring the right mind. And we explain in many ways what the principles of happiness are. By reading chapters three and four carefully, many people will be able to correctly understand the gateway to Happy Science.

Chapter five, entitled "Believing the Age of the Sun Will Come," is a new message from me about our future's design and its movement toward the utopia that I mentioned in the first book of this Laws Series, *The Laws of the Sun*.

As these Truths spread, this world on Earth will surely change into God's utopian world. I call this age "The Age of the Sun." I want to dream without end and believe in the coming of the Age of the Sun. I hope that this book, *The Laws of Happiness*, will be useful for the ideal future.

Ryuho Okawa
Master and CEO of Happy Science Group
December 2003

CHAPTER ONE

HOW NOT TO BE UNHAPPY

Overcoming Your Fate

1

Whether You Feel Happy or Not Depends On You

Even One Million Dollars Cannot Guarantee You Happiness

In a book I published called *The Laws of Miracles*,[*] the first chapter is entitled "How to Change Your Fate." Because I spoke on this theme very briefly and theoretically there, I would like to talk about this theme in this chapter.

"How to Change Your Fate" is a very bold and confident chapter title, indeed. But will your fate really be changed? Your answer will depend on how you understand and practice what I said there. It is difficult to foretell how everyone will understand the abstract meaning of my words. The way they're understood varies from person to person, and to truly know how they will be taken, I would need to ask each person, one by one. But if I could put the meaning of that chapter title in simpler words, they would be, "Most people want to find out how not to be unhappy." So, in this chapter, I would like to look into the theme, "How Not to Be Unhappy."

_____
[*] Translator's Footnote: This is the literal translation of the Japanese title, *Kiseki No Ho*. See Ryuho Okawa, *Kiseki No Ho* [The Laws of Miracles] (Tokyo: IRH Press, 2001). Available in the Japanese edition only.

There is the question of "When do we human beings feel most unhappy?" The sense of unhappiness we feel and the causes of the unhappy feelings inside us change according to our age. They change as time flows, according to our circumstances, or according to our standing in society. We often talk about happiness and unhappiness, but there are no fixed conditions that will guarantee one or the other. That is why I cannot tell you, "Owning one million dollars will give you happiness, and without that you'll only have unhappiness." That is just not the way things are.

Take physical strength, for example. To most of us, physical strength generally means happiness and physical weakness generally means unhappiness. But it also depends on the person and his or her circumstances. If it were true for everyone, the immense strength of a sumo wrestler's large physical build would give him nothing but happiness. But his physical body must also hamper him in his daily life. It must be years since he last woke up feeling light on his feet, and he must yearn to once again feel the lightness that others feel. Many commuters must feel unhappy about the heavily packed trains they have to take to work, and they must yearn to work at a place within walking distance from home. But once they retire and their legs are not as strong, they'll realize that being able to take the train is a source of happiness.

In this way, we can never really say, "If you have this, you are promised this outcome." You could be given the same circumstances, and the same thing could be happening to you, but the way you feel about them will change depending on your current position and how you see your situation.

Your Life's Theme Is Suited to You

Adults are not the only people who feel unhappy. In this modern age, children are also suffering from unhappiness. Children have to face a highly competitive world after all, but besides that, some of their worries stem from their parents' worries. Other children's worries result from their parents' limited work capabilities or lack of understanding of the world. And still other children's worries arise from their own nature.

In general, it is better if young children are surrounded by adults they can look up to, if possible. Adults have weak points and wrong sides that a child will surely notice. But the less a child sees adults' wrong sides and the more they see adults' admirable and ideal aspects, the better chance the child has of growing up smoothly.

However, after you have grown into adulthood, begun working in the real world, and started gaining various life experiences, the opposite is required. For your further growth to go smoothly, you'll need to recognize the shortcomings and weak points in both yourself and others to some extent. A too good-natured person sees the best in others. But to grow further as an adult with responsibilities, you'll need to recognize the flaws and weak points in yourself and others.

So, speaking generally, children develop more smoothly if they look up to adults and the majority of society becomes their teachers. Then, in the reverse position, when you are a teacher of others, the more you are aware of your own and other people's shortcomings and susceptibilities to mistakes, the more room you will have within yourself for further growth. Having this type of view is generally a good way of looking at your circumstances.

But the opposite is also true sometimes—for example, when children are raised by terrible parents. We see more of such parents nowadays. Many parents engage in child abuse, commit child neglect, act out in drunken violence, or are so financially deprived that they cannot sufficiently feed their children. Many such parents have various weak points and shortcomings in themselves.

So, increasing numbers of children are growing up while suffering from these worries, beginning with child abuse at home. When these children grow up, they carry these worries into adulthood unhealed, and this is why people from difficult childhood households have difficulty raising their own children in a healthy way.

Children going through this kind of childhood should think the opposite of what I mentioned earlier. During childhood, if you saw that your parents were terrible, there is only one decision to make in the end: resolve that you will not turn into your parents. Say to yourself, "I'm not going to be the same as my parents when I become an adult." If you keep thinking inside your heart, "I will be the opposite of them," you will steadily manifest it because this is the way things go in this world.

Because many people in the world recreate their childhood experiences in adulthood, if you've had many bad experiences during childhood, it is important that you do not carry them for the rest of your life. Instead, strive as much as possible to become the opposite of the kind of person your parents were. If, as a child, you saw adults suffering from the many wrongs and flaws inside themselves, promise yourself that you will not grow up like them. Children who observed various things and grew up recognizing the wrongs in the adults around them in this way are likely to become successful as adults by thinking to themselves, "I won't grow up that way," and practicing the opposite of those wrong actions.

Then, when you reach some level of success at work or in other real-world endeavors, you will receive a lot of praise, which will make it difficult to continue thinking and speaking badly of others. As you are praised more and more, you will start to notice that other people are good people.

Indeed, it is a mystery. But people who grow up noticing the flaws of the adults around them eventually grow up to recognize the opposite: the good within people. There are such actual cases. There are people who have grown up practicing the opposite of what surrounded them and have gone on to succeed in their lives.

Therefore, in general, children have smoother childhoods when the adults around them seem ideal, capable, and admirable because as small children, their understanding of the world is still slight.

However, the opposite also holds true. If the adults in your life are in a bad condition, you can become successful anyway through practicing the opposite by promising not to become like them in the future.

Conversely, if you were brought up in fortunate childhood circumstances, you will see this good fortune become the cause of your later mistakes. In this case, the essential next step is to study the evils of life. In other words, study the things we human beings are apt to get wrong, the commonly made human errors, the likely human pitfalls. Neglecting to do this would deprive you of a continuous source of further growth.

Very few people see their fortunate circumstances continue to the ends of their lives. So, if your childhood environment was favorable and the people around you seemed splendid, you are now required to take the next step: to study some of the world's human sufferings. Then, the more deeply you study the inadequacies in yourself and others, the more clearly the next thing you need to do will appear. This will become an essential factor in your next success.

So, it is essential to begin by knowing that there are no fixed conditions that can guarantee happiness or unhappiness to you. In various teachings, such as invincible thinking, I have taught many people about that. Your happiness or unhappiness does not come from a fixed form. It depends on what you learn from life's lessons and how you change the way you live.

I have also taught that life is a workbook of problems, and it is essential to know that each person has a different way of finding the answers to his or her problems from this workbook. Each person is given the theme of life that is suited to him or her.

2

The Seeds of Success Are Hiding within Failures

Why the Greatest Happiness Can Become the Greatest Suffering

During adulthood, your feelings of misery and inferiority gradually strengthen, and many of you who consciously think about these feelings believe that you are unhappy. You are saying to yourself, "I'm unhappy because I have this flaw. It's the reason why I can't be happy," "I can't be happy because of this worry I have," and "I'm unhappy because I can't escape from this inferiority complex." These thoughts might indeed be true from a subjective standpoint, but in many cases, they are not objectively the truth. I say this because people who are aware of their weak points and where they are apt to make mistakes have the advantage of being able to easily see what they must do to improve. Such people can clearly understand the things they need to do. When confronted with their mistakes and faults, they don't require another person's assistance to find out what they did wrong and what they need to do now. They don't require any "tutor" to help them.

So, when you make a mistake, it is natural to feel confused and suffer, but within this suffering, the seeds of your next success are already sprouting. The materials you are to learn from are contained within your mistake, where the next thing you must do is already being revealed to you. It is essential to look in this way at your mistakes.

In some sense, there is nothing to be feared more than continual success. This is because your present success contains the seed of your next failure, but you often don't realize this at the time. It is difficult to recognize the seed at that point. But often when you look back to that time after 5 to 10 years, you can see where that seed of failure began to sprout.

In this sense, even though being successful is a happy thing, you must keep in mind that success contains within it something fearful. It blocks from your view the seeds of your future mistakes and shortcomings. Success can overshadow your mistakes and shortcomings, hiding them from your recognition. Then, if you make a mistake later in your life, you will look back and see that the seed of it was almost always planted during good times. But during the good times, you just did not notice the seed of your later mistake. It's most essential to bear these things in mind.

For instance, most politicians hope to become prime minister at least once in their lives. But if they succeed at this, they may wake up one morning to find criticism about them written all over the newspapers, encouraging them to quit. It's an almost unbearable situation. The situation may not feel very real to you as an example because almost all of you have not experienced this kind of situation before, but please imagine that you are the prime minister. Imagine that all the newspapers have written criticisms about you, starting from the front pages and sometimes in huge letters. You turn on the television, and you hear yourself being criticized there too. You open a magazine, and you see that the magazine is criticizing you as well. It would probably make you wonder how so many people in this world could be so evil. You might ask yourself in shock, "Is speaking ill of people the only thing they're capable of doing? Are there this many people in the world making a living by speaking ill of others?" But it is the cost of success. It is the result of suddenly rising to the level of prime minister before being adequately prepared.

All politicians may hope to become prime minister someday, but failing to achieve this position can lead to happiness, at times. Because you are unable to achieve this position, there is no need to suffer censure and you are allowed to act freely. Even being an important cabinet minister will bring you criticism for shockingly small matters. So you would suffer even more severe circumstances if you became the prime minister.

In the end, you need to change your self-recognition. Because you feel like you are still the same person, you might not understand why people have changed their opinions about you. But when you attain a new position, you'll need to become a person suited to that position. You need to look ahead at the future person you'll need to become. If you do not prepare yourself in this way, you'll later find that this lack of preparation has led to suffering.

To become prime minister is the greatest happiness for a politician. It is the successful fulfilment of one's sense of mission. But this time of the greatest happiness can become a time of greatest suffering under a storm of arrows. You can find yourself in circumstances beyond your comprehension.

In this way, the seed of your next failure is embedded within your current path to success, but usually you do not recognize this. You are continually met with situations that make you think, "So many things have gone well, even though I'm just an ordinary person. I really managed to get very far in spite of that." But in actuality, this thought inside you, "I succeeded, even though I'm an ordinary person," is the seed of your unhappiness to come.

What this means is that as you walk up the stairs of success, you cannot remain an ordinary person. You cannot stay ordinary. You are required to become more capable than ordinary people with each step you take up the stairs.

So then what can you do to become a capable person? You will require more knowledge than others, a higher perspective, and further experience. In addition, it is essential to understand not just your thoughts and feelings but also the way other people are thinking. What are the other politicians thinking? What are people in the mass media thinking? What do the people of your country see? You had been paying attention to the voters in your district, but now you must also understand what other voters are feeling and broaden your perspective in this way. It is a broader view than you possessed before, but unless you are able to gain this broadness of perspective, you will struggle to endure under your new self-image, and a strong sense of unhappiness will grow in you.

Shedding Your Old Self Is Essential to Continued Success

I've used politicians and prime ministers as easily understandable examples. But if you are a CEO, a school teacher, or another kind of person, the same words hold true. As human beings, we all wish to succeed. This wish to succeed is our wish to advance beyond our present position, to rise above our present place by one or two steps. But as you go upward, so does the weight you must bear and the severity of people's eyes on you. Indeed, you are the person you have always been; that is true. Of course, you are an extension of who you've been up to this day, but there is another side as well. When you surpass some obstacle, you are not the same person anymore. You are not yourself anymore. You become a different person.

People who are unable to realize that they need to shed their skin will find that their success becomes their future suffering. Almost all ten thousand employees in a company are probably eager to become the CEO. But not even one out of a thousand will succeed at doing so. So, failing to become the CEO is where their happiness lies.

But almost everyone talks about the unhappy side of this failure. When someone else fills this position, they envy this person's luck and see their failure to get this position as unhappiness. But being the CEO can also be an unhappy thing. When the economy was growing, everything your company did worked out successfully. You as the CEO were only required to be at your desk all the time. Now, during the economy's slow growth and deflation and the turbulent age we have entered, being a person with responsibility is extremely difficult. It means that your company's employees can sleep peacefully through their nights while you suffer sleepless nights as the CEO. Truly, it is a miserable position to be in.

Back then, during the old times in Japan, high-ranking government officials in their fifties were allowed to step down and hop from one company to another while being paid a retirement salary. It was a much-admired position to be in. But now, what's awaiting them is misery, even if there are companies to step down to. Before, all they had to do was be at their desks.

But that's not sufficient anymore. Now they have to make decisions even though they are not experts in their field. But they cannot figure out what are the right decisions, so they suffer. It's impossible for someone who suddenly came to the company from outside to make the same kind of decisions that would only be possible by an expert with decades of experience working there, who had earned that position.

Because of these kinds of situations, we've seen no end to the number of deaths by suicide through hanging among such people who had expected this time in their lives to be easy. Others wonder what could possibly have caused these people to take their own lives when they'd achieved such important positions. In the end, their reasons were work-related problems that they couldn't solve. Unlike before, when all they had to do was show up, they were now required to make difficult decisions. These were decisions that would cause the entire company to go down if they failed, and they would never be forgiven by society. In the end, they could not bear the thought of suffering such severe public criticism.

When these people assumed their new position, they thought they were the same people as they were before. When they climbed that additional step up the stairs of success, they thought they would be living the easy life. Instead, they found themselves lying on a bed of needles. It is something we have often seen happen, and it is a fearful thing.

The Causes of Your Worries Encourage Further Self-Growth

During times of success, it's quite difficult to recognize that you are sowing the seeds of failure to come. The growing pride of being successful might also numb your ears to other people's input.

In this sense, it is a happy thing to have shortcomings and weak points or, in other words, to always be aware of these things in yourself. The saying, "People with a slight ailment are more careful about their health," is true. When something is physically wrong with you, you will take better care of your health, which will result in longevity. On the contrary, if you are healthy, tireless, and so strong that working all through the night doesn't affect you, there is a greater danger. The same holds true if you are aware of your shortcomings and weak points in your thirties, forties, or even fifties. You will know to not overstrain yourself. After all, these shortcomings and weak points are indeed indications that you still have room within yourself for continued growth.

You may, at times, have the seeds of several worries inside you, but it's better to think of them as the seeds that will also encourage you to develop. So, for example, it's a good thing to be in your sixties or your seventies and suffer from an inferiority complex about your intelligence. At that age, many people would have given up overcoming their complex a long time ago. So, you can be thankful to be in your sixties or your seventies and still be thinking to yourself, "Oh, I haven't been learning enough," "My level of ability is so low," and, "I haven't been thinking deeply enough," and still be suffering from a complex for such reasons because this itself indicates that you are exceptional. It means you are not completely satisfied with yourself and that there is room within you for further growth.

So, the more you learn and gain a variety of experiences, the more you will recognize that the seeds of your next success and development are contained in contradictions. For example, in your youth, you have boundless physical energy and very exceptional sensibility. Youths have keen sensitivity but not a lot of knowledge or experience—that is their weak point.

Then, what happens as you grow older? Undoubtedly you will physically weaken. You might also guess that your keenness of sensibility will fade. Nerves are apt to thicken, making you less open to sensing things. In this way, a very characteristic quality of being a youth fades in prominence, and in its place, your store of experience and knowledge grows. In this way, things get replaced by their opposites. In your youth, you could endure endless overstrain, but it becomes harder to do that after the age of 40.

At that point, you must find a way to continue working without overstraining yourself. This is the meaning of your knowledge and experience. It is not possible to work with the energy you had as a youth.

Next, your youthful sensibility also steadily vanishes. What can you do about this? When you encounter work and ideas that require the sensitivity of heart, you can delegate them to young people.

In this way, you are required to think according to your age. And developing the opposite of your current most active ability is what will most encourage and nurture your later growth. So, if your strongest point is having a lot of physical energy, then later on you'll be required to have not physical power but intelligence and experience. This is one example.

Then, when your intelligence grows, what will happen next? Your willpower sometimes weakens. You might wish that you were a better learner and could be more knowledgeable about a variety of things. But too much knowledge makes it difficult to make a decision and take action; as a result, you become less brave and suffer from indecision and inaction. Your courageous spirit wanes. The intellectual type is apt to be weak-willed. So, building a strong will is essential for this type of person.

The opposite of this type of person is a strong-willed person. A strong will, in some sense, means stubbornness, not paying attention to other people's opinions, and thinking steadfastly about having your own way. It's a strong point in you, but it can also become your weak point. To continue to spiritually grow, you will be required to develop your intellect to compensate for this weak point.

In this way, most of the reasons you will succeed have to do with your strong points, I'm sure. But if you look at the opposite of these strong points, you will often find hints about how to continue succeeding in the future. You must always remember this. Inside the opposites of your strengths, you shall find the seeds to guide you in the future.

As I've described before, many religious people are apt to be very spiritual people. It is indeed true that you can only bring things such as your mind, your thinking, and your soul back to the other world. The other world doesn't include material things, it's true. But there are many people who are living too spiritually in this world, who are too idealistic in their tendencies. These people are often at the risk of finding themselves falling into one of this earthly world's traps. If you are this type of person, you will see a huge difference in yourself if you put a little effort into learning a little about worldly things, gaining more worldly knowledge and perspective, and adopting practical thinking.

If you are the opposite type of person, the one who can only believe in rational and practical things, this probably has become your bottleneck and is leading to conflicts between you and other people. In this case, I suggest cultivating a little more sensitivity of heart for mystical things. If you can open your heart and have a little more curiosity about the things you have not accepted before, you will see new aspects of things and your relationships with other people will change.

In some sense, life's progress is a journey of self-growth. Each of you has been opening your path to success by taking advantage of some strong point in yourself; at the same time, you have been suffering from your weak points. But on your journey of self-expansion, you must find the seed of your next strong point hidden within your weak points, or there can be no upward step in your personal growth, self-expansion, or self-development. In addition, you must keep in mind that contained inside your strong points is the next hole you could fall into. If you don't keep this in mind, it will be difficult for you to advance one step forward in your journey to become a wiser person.

There is immense power contained in keeping on thinking. This power can only be known by the people who practice it in their real lives. It is possible to let each of your days pass you by while thinking of nothing at all. But the great power contained within deeply thinking and weaving new ideas becomes ever more knowable the more you practice such thinking in real life. You will see the same phenomena occurring with you as in martial arts: the more you diligently practice it, the more you will see your capabilities grow.

3

Life Is a Journey of Self-Discovery

The Two Purposes of Life in This World

The first purpose of our life in this world is the journey of self-discovery we undergo. The reason we are born with a personality itself means that we are here in this world to master our lives—to look inside ourselves and discover the reason we have the personality that we do and what kind of life we were given to live. Life is a journey of looking inside ourselves—a journey of self-discovery—from which no one can escape.

Another purpose of living this earthly life concerns our interrelations with other people. What kind of role can we fulfill in relation to people and society? Through our experiences related to others, we learn about our own selves as well as how important it is that we influence one another as we live together. These are the two fundamental purposes of the lives we live in this world.

If there was no one else in the world and you were living here alone, it would be very difficult to learn about yourself. Thanks to the numerous people with various views and ways of thinking as well as the people that you like and dislike to various degrees, you can learn who you are. Through these differences, you can notice your unbalanced ways of thinking and recognize whether you are close to the general standard.

So, you indeed cannot push others to be as you would like them to be. But these variously different types of people are something to be thankful for. When you see certain types of people, certain ways of thinking, and certain personalities, their existence can seem to be a huge mystery to you. But these essential talents and personalities can shed light on yourself and help you understand yourself. We are living in this world with one another for this purpose.

Because learning about yourself is not possible without other people's existence, God gave us this world where we polish each other as relative existences. By allowing us to live in this world, He lets us deepen our self-recognition and experience the joy of having possibilities within ourselves. This is the purpose God gave to this world.

The World that God Sees

When you make further progress in your religious mind, you will begin to recognize something. There are two eyes (and this is also taught in Buddhism) that I call the differentiating eye and the equality eye, and both of these eyes greatly develop over the course of your life.

What is the differentiating eye? This is the eye that clearly sees how very numerous are the differences among people or, for example, the differences between people's talents. The more progress you are able to make in your spiritual training, the more clearly you will see these differences. With immense clarity, you recognize the wide differences between people's innate abilities— the gifts they are born with. You recognize the differences in human existence, the differences in the qualities people are born with, and the differences in how their divine nature manifests. This is the differentiating eye.

You will learn about that, but at the same time, the other eye, the eye of equality, will grow. Within you, a recognition of many different existences will grow; at the same time, with this other mysterious eye of equality, you will see the many different existences surrounding you combine as one and appear in your eyes as equal existences. You will see the equal value that each of their lives has, in spite of your recognition of the great human differences.

Through the eye of equality, you will see that all other living existences, such as animals and plants, also possess shining lives and are undergoing the same training of their souls. It is a mystery you will not have words to describe. You will come to feel the hearts of animals and plants. You will see that they are all training their souls and living out their lives in society. It is a mysterious experience, indeed. Animals also are building families and going through struggles to obtain their food. They are also working to take on different roles, such as those that handle difficult things and those that assist them.

Your recognition of such various things will grow, and you will attain this eye that sees the equality of all living existences. When these two contradicting eyes—the differentiating eye and the equality eye—combine within you, they become like the eyes of God. God sees through both types of eyes.

In Japanese, the word *jihi*, which means "compassion," is sometimes called *daihi*, which means "great sadness." To this large eye of great sadness, the suffering figures of various living existences, all living things, and all of life in this world, which are earnestly living despite their suffering, will appear. You will see each of the shining figures of these living existences, from small animals to highly evolved human beings, each bearing a suffering and sadness of its own and all living on this planet Earth together. It is a very sad but, at the same time, very warm sight. They appear bearing sadness, but also, they appear full of hope and brightness.

In truth, you cannot profess to have entered the world of enlightenment without having developed these contradicting eyes. On your way up the stairs to this gate to enlightenment, you will polish one of the two eyes: the differentiating eye or the equality eye. At the same time, there are times when you must surpass the vision of that eye and polish the other eye. The effort to integrate these contradicting eyes leads us up the stairs of enlightenment. This is also the reason this earthly world is not self-completing and is connected to the other world.

4

The Change in Your Self-Recognition Is Success for Your Soul

To Recognize Your Limit Is to Overcome It

In the course of your life, you will surely face many worries and sufferings. But please see them as things to be thankful for. With an earnest heart, you must know that they are things to be grateful for. If there were nothing to worry you, it would mean that you have no room for development. So, you might face problems that cannot be solved, but within these problems lies the infinite possibility of development.

You don't need to regret a life of many mistakes. Hidden within your mistakes are the seeds of the next creation, the seeds of your further growth. You must know that creating this change, expansion, and growth in your self-recognition is, in truth, growing your very soul. The creation of this change in your self-recognition is, in truth, the spiritual success of your soul; this is the reason you have been born to this earthly world with bodies, have been living many decades since you were a baby—growing through the years and aging—and will then pass away from this world. This is

THE LAWS *of* HAPPINESS

something you must know. You must know that this change in your self-recognition is the true essence of enlightenment.

I, myself, have undergone many changes in my self-recognition. I began publishing spiritual messages in 1985, and I remember that after I had completed three of them—*The Spiritual Message from Nichiren*, *The Spiritual Message from Kukai*, and *The Spiritual Message from Jesus Christ*—I felt a sense of having accomplished enough. I felt that my mission was complete. I thought to myself, "Now that I've taught others this much about the Truths, it's enough to give meaning to my having been born into this world at this time. Even if I were to die now, I've finished most of my work here. What I've now accomplished is enough, I'm sure of that; I've taught people about the other world's existence and the existence of the other world's spiritual beings, and I've also published a spiritual message from Jesus Christ. To take on more than that would become a tremendous task." I had not foreseen, at that time, the continual increase of my work to its scale today.

It was not the end of my work. When I thought my work had ended, more and more work continued to appear. There came more and more work to do. When I thought to myself that I had finished, more tasks came one after another in a never-ending continuation.

I thought that my work had finally confronted its limit, but what came after that was beyond my own limit. Surprisingly, the breakthrough I made came when I recognized my limit. Indeed, it is surprising, but you break through your limits right at the moment when you think you have come to the end of your ability and cannot see anything more that you can do. Just when you feel that you have made so many mistakes that you have nothing more to give, you will break through your limits.

This means that you cannot break through your limits without reaching that point of struggle when you finally begin to search for other possible routes or ways of thinking. The solution appears in your struggle to find it. After putting out three spiritual messages, I had thought that my work was complete. Even now, I think to myself on a yearly basis that my work is complete. Every year, I think that there is nothing more to teach. But, by a true mystery, the next work appears to me.

I thought about the reason that this happens and what the difference between now and before could be. The difference has been in the reaction I receive from people. There are many unseen reactions from the people who receive my thoughts and teachings. And I believe that I have been changing myself according to these reactions.

So, when I was around thirty years old, I believed myself to be doing well physically and intellectually. I saw that I had physical strength and very quick thinking. I believed that I knew about everything and that I'd have an answer for everything.

But after I got a little older, I gradually recognized that there were many things I did not know about. How this happened was indeed a mystery. However, I steadily saw more and more things I had not known about, and I was thinking to myself, "I don't know about this. I don't know about that. And I don't have confidence regarding this subject, either. What should I do?"

Why did this happen? The group of people I was speaking to had changed. At the beginning, when I had just started this work of Happy Science, I was mostly speaking to a small group of people who were drawn to spiritual things out of curiosity, and it felt like enough if I was able to make them happy. That was what this group of people was seeking, too. I don't think they were necessarily looking for more than that.

However, when I reached some level of recognition in society and the group of people I was speaking to expanded, various other types of people appeared, including those from other countries. Many kinds of people were reading my books and listening to my lectures, and my audience gradually expanded. Because of this, when I thought about the reactions I was receiving from them, I gradually began to feel that there were more things that I did not know about. I thought, "There are this kind of people now, and that kind of people also. And even this new kind of person is learning my teachings now." I gradually recognized more things I did not yet know about, and that worried me and made me think to myself, "I need to do something about this."

So, at the beginning of my work, I believed myself to have enough knowledge, enough enlightenment, enough mental spirit, and enough physical strength. But as I grew older, I gradually began to recognize that this was not enough, and I began to lose confidence in myself. But I found that when I thought I was finished with my work, I usually developed another level. It was truly amazing.

Recognizing Your Shortcomings Means that You're in a Time of Growth

It might be something difficult to realize about yourself, but it is very easy to do when you look at yourself in relation to others. It is because of what I explained to you earlier in this chapter, when I said, "Children will do better if they see adults as splendid people. Even if the adults have shortcomings and weak points, it is better to look at those less and to look very closely at only the splendid aspects. This will help the children grow more quickly." I said that, and I could say the same thing about this religious organization when it was in its childhood. When I started Happy Science, other already existing religious organizations appeared splendid. And I thought, "They're doing really great work. They're publishing so many books, and they seem to have many members, too. They're recognized so much by society. They're really splendid. I hope we can grow into one like them soon."

I gradually worked while thinking this, and one day, there came a point in time when I began recognizing the weak points and shortcomings of several religious organizations. I saw things such as, "This area of their teachings is a bit of a weak point for them," "The way they operate their organization also has a shortcoming in this area," and, "Their religious leader isn't experienced enough in this area and doesn't know what to do. He or she must not have knowledge about this subject." In this way, I could not help noticing these things.

It was when I started noticing their weak points that I began to surpass them. It happened at that exact moment. Then, when Happy Science had progressed far beyond other religious organizations, I could see everything in the palms of my hands. I could see each religious organization's way of thinking, teachings, behavioral patterns, and weak points, and I could even see what they should do to resolve their weak points. When they appeared in my eyes as a far-off goal to aspire to, I could not see their shortcomings at all. They only appeared splendid in my eyes. It was just when we were beginning to surpass them that I began to very clearly see their weak points.

When you start to see others' shortcomings, you might wonder if you have become a terrible person to be doing so, but it is a result of having reached a higher perspective that enables you to very clearly see their mistakes and limits.

I experienced this again and again. So, I was not necessarily criticizing other religious organizations in an intentional way, but when I did speak of them critically, it was usually at the points in time when Happy Science was on the verge of surpassing them. I was not trying to speak of them badly. It showed that I was then capable of seeing the shortcomings of their teachings and operations, and because I was noticing them, I could not help but mention them.

When I completely surpassed other organizations, I stopped mentioning their shortcomings because, at that point, they did not draw my attention. The same thing happens to you as an individual. When you can easily recognize your shortcomings, weak points, and mistakes, this indicates that you are on the verge of shedding your current self—because you would not be able to notice these things unless you had reached the point of abandoning your old self. People who feel satisfied with who they are now are unable to see their shortcomings and weak points. And if they do see them, they wish to somehow hide them from being noticed by others. They want to cover them up with something and try to gloss over them with their strong points.

So, please know that when you start to easily recognize your shortcomings and weak points, this indicates that this is a time of climbing one step above where you used to be. People who think they have been errorless have in truth made various mistakes. They just have not recognized them. If you notice your ability to recognize mistakes becoming keener, you'll often be able to foresee your mistakes before making them.

5

How To Change Your Fate

Recognize Your Soul-Tendency to Foresee Your Fate

In this section, I would like to discuss the subject of human fate. If someone were to ask me if there exists such a thing as human fate, my answer from my experience of many accumulated years working as a religious leader would be, "Yes, it exists." But when I say that such a thing as fate exists, I don't mean that there is a fixed story. I am referring to the soul-tendency we each have that to a large degree forecasts the type of life we will be leading. This is why my answer would, indeed, be that human fate exists after all.

By examining a person's soul-tendency, it is possible to generally forecast what sort of successes and failures that person will experience. Even though these events are probably 5, 10, or 20 years in the future, or even in the twilight years of your life, by looking at your soul-tendency, you can foresee what may happen. This is why I would say that human fate exists—in this meaning of the term.

But there is also a way to overcome your fate. If you examine yourself and others with the heart of study, looking closely at the soul-tendencies, strong points, and weak points of yourself and others with the wish to change yourself and shed your old self, then your fate will change. This is my answer.

If your fate is an unhappy and terrible one that you wish to avoid suffering, there is only one way to escape it and that is by having a clear grasp of your soul-tendency. If you clearly understand your soul-tendency, then you'll see your future fate. And now that you can see ahead into the future, you will know what you must do. Because you'll be able to picture what will happen to you, you'll be able to avoid the dangers.

You will also need to develop new abilities. Work on developing new strengths from your current weak points, the same way you discover the seed of your next mistake from within your current strong points. In this way, you can keep achieving continual success.

Abandoning Excessive Worldly Desires Leads to Happiness

In this sense, fate exists; but it is also possible to find and improve your fate. However, I think you will also find that some fates are unchangeable, no matter how you may try. For this type of fate, I recommend that you stop trying to change it. I believe that half of human life's sufferings come from desiring things beyond our means. Human beings desire self-growth, and that is a desire that we cannot completely live without. But half of human desires are beyond our reasonable limits.

To know your fate means to know your life's mission and to also know your limits. Even the Devil cannot easily destroy those who understand their own limits in talent, personality, and physical strength. It is very difficult to fool or trap someone who is aware of their own limits and means. But with someone who is not aware of them, it is easy. All that the Devil has to do is dig a hole in front of that person. It doesn't take any effort or thought for the Devil to do this. He only needs to dig a hole in the ground a few meters ahead and wait for you to walk right into it. It is as easy as that. This will happen to you if you simply assume that your ability is limitless.

Human beings do have limitless possibility, but they also have limits generated by their soul-tendency. To break through this inner limit, you must observe the weak points and strong points in yourself and others, and you must make a study of your life's journey by continually comparing yourself with others. But some limits will still be unconquerable, and in regard to these, you must think about controlling your desire. Failure does not come to those who know that success beyond one's own ability leads to failure.

Too much worldly desire is called an "attachment," and abandoning this attachment will make you happier. This path to happiness is open to all people. So, when it comes to your desires, it is best to assume that about half of them are excessive.

I mentioned in the second section of this chapter that most politicians will be happier if they don't become prime minister and could become less happy if they do become prime minister. The same holds true for other people. Even if you are unable to achieve your wish to become something, there are cases when you will be happier as a result.

For example, if you don't become an ideal housewife, you might be happier devoting yourself to your career. Also, some parents think that their own unhappiness is caused by their children's poor grades in school. But there are cases of families who are unhappy because their children are so intelligent that it is impossible for the parents and children to understand each other. In this way, limits don't exist but at the same time do exist, and limits exist but at the same time don't exist. It is the way of this world.

Look at Yourself through Others' Eyes

One day, before I became well-known and when I had more freedom to walk outside, I passed by a mom-and-pop grocery store on my way home. The couple running this shop came out to greet me on the street, and it seemed their business was doing well. I noticed that they had a certain religion's motto hanging on their storefront. I won't say which religion it was, but they must have been believers of it.

Because they came outside to greet me, they gave me a very friendly impression. But when I saw their highly priced items, I decided not to buy anything. This couple was running their store very happily, and they were very friendly to their customers; so they were probably following their religion's teachings. But even though they were very humble, always smiling, and always thanking their customers, I didn't go there very often because of their high prices.

This is the limit of their religion's teachings that I recognized. Their religion is probably teaching their believers, "To create a prosperous business, you must always smile and be humble. It's important not to forget this attitude of mind."

Because human beings make rational judgments, they could be charmed into buying something from the couple's store once or twice; but it wouldn't continue forever. If there is a store with good products at lower prices just a few hundred meters down the street, there isn't anyone who would continue buying from a store just because the owners are friendly. They might buy from them for their charm once in a while but not continually.

This grocery store is probably still running at the same scale of business as they did back then. The reason their business has not grown in scale is that they don't have quite enough of practical thinking.

In this way, you create your own limits, but they are delineated by the objective evaluations of other people. In a this-worldly sense, these evaluations might be the result of competition—the objective evaluations of other people are setting a limit you are not able to overcome. Therefore, when you think that you are making the best efforts you can but your path does not open, you need to add an objective eye.

One perspective is that it may be better overall if you do not achieve much growth. If you feel that your happiness lies in running a mom-and-pop grocery store at the same scale, generation after generation, this is a happy life in itself. You may feel more meaningfulness in your life by being happy with the current scale of your business and devoting yourself to other areas of your life, such as religious activities. This is also a splendid life in itself. But if you are someone who wishes to enlarge the scale of your business a little more and grow it into a supermarket, then you might not feel completely happy keeping your business at its current level.

Which you choose is up to each of you. But if you feel that you have been making your best efforts but the path has not opened for you, it is important to think from the customer's or outside person's standpoint.

Think Continually Regarding the Limit You Are Facing

The same holds true when spreading the Truths. Some of the members of Happy Science who are spreading the Truths may feel unhappy that they have not been successful. Some of the members wonder, "These are such great teachings. I wonder why I'm not succeeding." Actually, the people they are talking to are thinking in their hearts, "I think I would become a member if someone more splendid would recommend it to me, but I don't want to join if it's this person." So they respond by saying, "I'm happy with my life already, so no, thank you."

As you make efforts to spread the Truths, if you are confronted by a wall and find yourself wondering, "The teachings are so wonderful. Why won't more people believe in them?" try looking at yourself from the other person's perspective.

My books are being read by a tremendous number of people, but there are also many people who have not read them yet. Among these people, some think that they are happy enough believing in another religion, and others feel happy enough without reading religious books. Still, some others feel that believing in a religion would only make them unhappy. There may be biased views in them, but we are required to think of a way to guide such people and of how this should be done.

It is a religious Truth that spiritual beings exist, the other world exists, and God exists. But there are hundreds of millions of people in the world who cannot believe in them or choose not to believe in them. To change a world such as this, tremendous energy is required, and we cannot succeed at this so easily. We are required to be persistent and also to carry out our activities widely. To break through our limits, we need to look at things from the opposite side's standpoint and also be aware of the opposite side's perspective.

Then, when you're unable to break through your limit, there is also a meaning behind this. So, it is important to continually think about what to do about it. The next step for your further growth lies in continual thinking.

Happy Science is a religion that will continue to grow much, much more. I am on the path of continued growth; at the same time, the members who are learning and joining in this movement of Happy Science are also on the path of continued growth. My wish is to establish this kind of culture of limitless growth. I will be glad if this chapter's hints inspire you to have more interest in your soul's growth.

CHAPTER TWO

ONE STEP UP IN YOUR WORK CAPABILITY

Four Ways to Become More Capable

1

Devote Your Life to Your Divine Calling

Feel Passionate about Your Work

Probably many people wish to become more capable in their work, but they're suffering because they haven't found a way. Such people are men and women from all walks of life, from the new employee to the corporate CEO. I've written this chapter to serve as a useful guide for all of these readers. This is my purpose for discussing the topic, "One Step Up in Your Work Capability," which is also the title of this chapter.

There is a simple litmus test to tell if you will become more capable in your work as time goes on. It's to check whether you feel passionate about your work. Without this passion within you, you're unlikely to become a capable person in your work. Some people with innate, inborn talent could still do well in a disagreeable job. Usually, however, people don't endure in this type of job for very long even if they do well in the beginning. As time goes on, their dislike for it gradually grows stronger, they eventually do worse in their jobs, and they stop being recognized for their work. As a result, they eventually leave their job. The feeling of passion for your work is extremely important for this reason.

To put it another way, it means to find the purpose that you live for. Your work continues over the course of your whole lifetime. Going through college takes three or four years of your life, perhaps six years at the most. But the time you spend in your work lasts for decades. With the number of career changes rising, people work in different jobs over the course of their lives, nowadays. But to change jobs as many as tens of times in your life, you would have to be a very easily bored person. Normally, a person spends his or her whole life working at one job or, at most, two or three kinds of jobs. In this sense, your work is your means of making a living over a very long period of your life. So, you will be very unhappy if your work is not your divine calling, the destiny you were born to live, or the life plan that you set up before you were born into this world. If this were your situation, being born into this life wouldn't be so worthwhile. Nevertheless, there are people among us who are working in jobs that aren't in their original life plan.

When you look quietly inside yourself, if you feel a sense of passion and calling for your work and a feeling welling up saying that you've been born to do this work, then this work is, indeed, the work that's suited to you. You're very likely to succeed if this is true for you. On the other hand, if your current job is one that you're itching to leave, you won't become very successful in it even if you force yourself to keep going. Also, some people who are working in jobs they aren't suited to already know what kind of job is perfect for them. If this is the case with you, it's clear that you're not in the job you belong in, and you should consider a career change. But please bear in mind that there are also people who dislike working in the first place, and these people have very little chance at succeeding, no matter what they do. Society contains a certain percentage of such people.

In the end, to advance one step up in your work capability, first you're required to feel passionate about your work. That means feeling deeply that this work will bring your calling to fruition, fulfill the destiny you were born with. If you have thoughts that say, "Through this work I can be of service to the world; I can do something for the world in repayment. Through my work I will accomplish self-realization and live in devotion to other people and the world," then, you will steadily become more capable in your work.

But if this is not the way you're able to think about your work, and instead, you think of it basically as a temporary job, you won't become highly capable. If you think, "I'm not interested in getting better at my work; but I want to get a higher salary every year. I'll be happiest if I'll get a raise every year, even if I don't become highly capable at what I do," there is almost no possibility for you to become capable in your work. Feeling passionate about your work means that through your occupation, you're able to let the meaning of your birth into this world come to fruition.

It's important to feel in your heart that through your current work, you're contributing something to the world. It can be called your sense of mission. There is a huge difference between people with a sense of mission in their work and people without one. Those without a sense of mission who are trying to get through the world making easy gains won't understand you, even if you lecture them. In response, there is not much you can say to people like that other than, "You'll have to judge the results for yourself at the conclusion of your life." What's important, first, is to feel passionate about your work. Through your work, you must try to find the meaning of having been born into this world, of living this life, which lies behind the passion you feel for your work.

Give Your Best in Your Current Circumstances

Your current employer might not have been the top choice on your list when you were searching for a job. Perhaps there were paths in other places you were hoping to take, and you had other employers' names on your list, but you were hired by your current one after your first and second choices turned you down. So, you might currently be working at the third, or even the fifth employer on your list. Or perhaps your current employer wasn't on your list at all, but you accepted a position with them because one happened to open up. There are different possible scenarios.

But in the world, only a few people succeed at getting hired by the employer of their choice. These people didn't necessarily apply for the job fully believing that it was their life's destiny to work at that organization. Many applied to their top-choice employers because of these employers' strong reputation, good name recognition, or high-paying positions, and not necessarily because they were born with a calling to work at those places. Perhaps they chose their employers because their friends were aiming to get into those companies or they were places that received high popularity ratings among people. For this type of person, whether to make their current job their forever job might not be such a serious question. If this is the case with you, your guardian spirits, guiding spirits, or high spirits of heaven might not have a constructive reason to support you. Heavenly beings won't have a reason to strongly support people who have chosen their employers based purely on their worldly reputation.

These days, it's important for many people working for corporate employers to believe that they were led to their companies by a destined connection and that they received a divine calling to work there whether it was their first choice or not. With a mindset that says, "I came here by a destined connection and was divinely called to be here," they'll rapidly progress to higher positions, succeed in those positions, and become capable of working in the way they had hoped to work. As a result, they'll live their lives in dedication to their divine calling.

But what would happen if there were workers at your company—your colleagues, subordinates, and superiors—who continually complained, saying, "I shouldn't have taken this job. I must have made some kind of mistake"? For example, if a new employee has been saying since day one on the job, "I don't know why I decided to work here," everyone working around them would probably say, "You're ruining our work environment, so please leave as soon as you can." Or, for example, what would happen if a senior staff member said to a newly hired and enthusiastic employee, "You shouldn't have come to such a terrible place to work. You probably made the wrong decision to take this job"? It would be sure to dampen the new employee's spirits.

Employees who complain like this have a harmful influence on the company. This is true even when they're entry-level employees, but the degree of harm increases the higher up you go. If such a person were in the position of a department manager, his or her influence could wreak great havoc on the company.

So, don't always concern yourself with other people's perspectives and opinions. Instead, it's essential to think to yourself, "Since I'm working in this company that I'm connected to by destiny, I will discover and accomplish my divine calling in this place." Even if you don't have a calling in this company, new doors won't open if you don't work earnestly, but a new path will open if you do. So, to begin with, it's essential to try to accomplish your calling in this place where you are currently working.

Some people have a strong love for their company. They're always thinking to themselves, "I'm currently working for a good company. The work I am doing there is good work." They're always saying to their parents, brothers, sisters, friends, and acquaintances, "It's a good place where I'm working now." These are the people who will be promoted to higher positions. But this is not the case for people who are always speaking ill of their company, assuming that other employees are not overhearing them outside the company. It's the same in any other organization. For example, say that you are a cram-school teacher, and you are pretending to work hard in the cram school. But after work, when you're out at a restaurant, coffee shop, or somewhere else, if you are telling people you meet, "I don't think coming to our cram school would help anyone pass the entrance exam," then you're doing the opposite of your mission. It would be wrong to be receiving a salary if you're thinking in this way. If you are saying, "I became a cram-school teacher by accident and just to earn a living. No one would pass the entrance exams by coming to our school," it isn't the right attitude toward your job even if these words are true. It would only be right to call it your profession if, in your mind, you believe that you are working to help your students pass their exams.

You need to think, "It doesn't matter where I'm working right now. It's through giving my best effort to this job that my divine calling will arise." People who can't think in this way seldom see themselves succeed. And, also, people who speak ill of their professions or workplaces have to ask themselves, "Is what I'm saying true? Could it be that I just dislike working? Could I just be lazy?"

Highly capable people show a certain degree of capability regardless of what kind of work they do. There is probably a job that they're especially suited for and that they believe is the job that would fit them best, but in a world with thousands of different jobs, it's very rare to be especially good at one job only and not good at anything else. In most cases, people who are highly capable at one job are very good at other jobs, too. For example, people who achieve great results selling rings and necklaces in a jewelry store also achieve great results selling women's clothing or cars, after they've learned the necessary technical information. This is often the way things are in professions.

What's important is to think, "I will put forth my best effort under these circumstances, and I will accomplish my calling from within them." Just by thinking this way, you'll become a different person than you were yesterday, and you'll become capable in your work starting today. Your path to success is to have this mindset inside yourself.

2

Paths to Self-Development

Work Capability Cannot Grow without Effort

The second point I'd like to talk about regarding stepping up your work capability is more specific. It's on the topic of self-development. You cannot ignore the importance of self-development if you want to become more capable in your work. For example, no one can become a swimmer without practicing swimming. Of course, to swim as well as a professional swimmer, your innate physical ability and physical build matter. Most people wouldn't be able to become an Olympic swimmer no matter how hard they practice. However, there is no question that even Olympic swimmers weren't good swimmers at the outset, before they started to practice.

Also, it wouldn't help if you tried to practice swimming on the ground. You'd have to practice in actual water to truly become capable of swimming. It's the same with learning English or a foreign language. You cannot learn to speak a foreign language without studying that language, no matter how intelligent you are. I can promise you that. How quickly you master the language may be different from others, but you won't become capable of speaking it unless you make the effort to study it. Whatever it is you do, if you make the effort to develop yourself in it, you'll become more capable than you are now, within the bounds of your given potential. If you compare yourself with more capable people and lament the difference, that is your choice. But those who are very good at that activity could be making hidden efforts that no one would ever realize from the outside. Foremost is this inner fight against yourself. In this sense, there is nothing that you cannot improve at by making an effort to develop yourself, whether it's your intelligence, your physical ability, your mind, or your religious enlightenment. Please know foremost that there is nothing that you cannot improve at through self-development, the inner fight against yourself.

Reading—Acquiring Information from Books and Newspapers

With the overall scope of people's work in mind, I would say that the most usual path to self-development is through reading. A large portion of everyone's reading material is books, but the newspaper is another reading material. Reading is a way to acquire information, like buying ingredients with which to cook. Without gathering the ingredients first, even an excellent chef wouldn't be able to prepare a dish. Depending on the chef's skills, there could be differences in how well a dish turns out, but without the ingredients, you wouldn't be able to cook anything to begin with, no matter who you are.

The same thing can be said about your work. Work is like cooking, after all. Day after day, you are "cooking" when you're manufacturing a car, writing a document, or doing anything else. For this reason, gathering information is a very important part of your job. One way to gather information is by reading. Through reading books and newspapers every day, you gather ideas to base your thinking on, or you gain useful materials for your work. To smoothly handle new work that comes to you daily, you have to constantly be gathering new materials.

So, reading is a basic part of your work. Speaking generally, many capable people are also avid readers. There is a 70 or 80 percent correlation between reading and capability at work. Of the people who read books and newspapers avidly, about 70 or 80 percent are also highly capable people at work. For one thing, these readers fervently gather information. But reading also makes them think faster, so it's normal for them to become highly capable people.

But there is a group of about 20 to 30 percent of avid readers who aren't very capable at their work. Some of them are the types who aren't good with human relationships. They may be the type of people who like to stay at home a lot to read, but their human relationships don't go smoothly, which makes it hard for their work to go smoothly. But there's also a way for this type of person to become successful. Even if your human relationships don't go smoothly, if you're an avid reader, there are other paths you can take to succeed as an individual.

Another type in this group is the type that reads by sheer habit, those who read just the words on the page. This type of person also has difficulty becoming capable at work. They go through books and newspapers like water running from a faucet, so they aren't capable of grasping the main points. The majority of avid readers who don't become capable in their work fall into this category. They're escaping into a world of written words because they feel like they always need to be doing something, and they can't stay still. They read books for this reason, but what they're actually doing is escaping from having to think and be creative.

Even if you read large quantities of things, such as newspapers, you could spend a lot of time at it, but it won't be meaningful unless you can make use of what you're reading. If you can find a useful point from the newspaper that you can use toward your work that day, you'll become capable in your work. But if you're only reading a lot simply to kill time, there's not much hope that it will help you become better.

In some cases, the issue could also be the contents of your reading material. In other words, some people are reading books or magazines that have no deeper value. They'll be able to chat about the latest gossip, but they won't become excellent at their work.

To sum up, among avid readers who aren't seeing their work improve, there are those whose human relationships don't go smoothly, those who are reading just by habit and not grasping the main points, and those whose reading materials have no deep value.

Those who read aimlessly should practice grasping the main points of the books they read. And when they finish one book, it's important to train themselves to think about what they learned from the book. It's important not to be forced by the author to read the book, but to truly read the book consciously. The author has many things he or she wants to say in the span of hundreds of pages. But the reader doesn't have exactly the same interests as the author, so it's important to remember to find the part, information, or idea that is useful to you. By developing an eye for determining what part of the book is useful, valuable, and impactful for you, you'll become more capable in your studies and your work.

Without the ability to digest the contents of a book, you'll only be letting the book persuade you. If you're not careful, you may end up reading something that was written persuasively but not understanding its contents, which means you're letting your time go to waste. A more specific suggestion I would make is to train yourself to underline or highlight the main points as you read them.

Writing—Sorting Through Your Problems

Writing is also an important method of self-development in these times. Being very busy, people nowadays might not have the time to write long compositions. What I advise is to write down the problems that you are facing to organize them. In these modern times, information comes from everywhere, and there are many other thoughts coming from within your own mind. Writing them down will often make things very clear to you.

Write down the problems you are facing, what you wish to tell people, what thoughts have just come to mind, and what you are trying to accomplish right now. When you're unable to make a decision and you're lost and feeling confused, you can often get clear on things by calming your mind, picking up a pencil, and writing them all down on a piece of paper. Try to stop yourself from saying, "I'm too busy," and take out a piece of paper and begin with writing down the issues at hand, your current aims, your current tasks or jobs, and what you want to tell your superior right now. It doesn't have to be long. It will be enough to jot these things down as notes. Just write them down on a sheet of paper and lay them all out.

When your mind is in a state of confusion, if you list the problems you're dealing with, it will help you organize them in a clear form. It will help you see what you should do, and then you can get each thing done, one by one, and that will resolve your problems. Many people fall into a panic when they're confused about problems. When two or three issues come up at the same time, a simple person tends to fall into panic. So, when you are struggling because you cannot find a way forward and don't know what to do, write the issues down on one sheet of paper. They can be written out as short notes. Try to organize your thoughts in this way. By writing them out, you'll begin a conversation with yourself, and you'll see clearly what the problems you are facing right now actually are. You'll become more capable in your work in this way.

In the morning, when you sit down at your desk at work, pick up a pencil, take out a memo pad, and write down what you need to do that day, what you will be working on today. You could make a list of three things. If you can write down the three things that are essential to do that day, you're already headed in a good direction. Doing this will help you work very efficiently throughout the day. But if you are the type who is going to work without a clear idea, pouring yourself some tea and thinking, "I wonder what I'll do today. I hope the phone will ring soon," you won't become capable at what you do. Therefore, in the morning, first write down your to-do list for that day.

Then, around six or eight o'clock when you've finished your work, take out a sheet of paper before leaving to go home and reflect on the work you've accomplished that day. Write these things down, and reflect on how well you worked on them. You could take this further and write down which ones are incomplete and determine whether you'll work on them tomorrow or next week. Doing this will clarify what you will need to do tomorrow. In this way, it's very important to clarify which work you've finished and which is ongoing. If you don't do this and instead work aimlessly, you won't have enough time to finish much at all. Time will just keep passing you by. People who can see clearly what they need to do that day and what they actually accomplished will see huge improvements in their daily work efficiency.

Listening—Gathering Information

In addition to reading and writing, listening is essential. Like reading, listening is a way to gather information and supply yourself with materials. The radio and television are some examples of sources to listen to. There are also DVDs and CDs. Television and videotapes are things to watch, but they are also things to listen to.

Listening is another one of the abilities we human beings possess. It is extremely important to gather information and acquire materials by using our sense of hearing. It's also important to listen to other people's stories. We should all think of our ears as an important tool. Our eyes are not the only tools we can use for work. Our sense of hearing is another tool we can use. During busy times, we also can use our senses of sight and hearing separately at the same time. For instance, watching television is something you can do while also reading a book. As you are reading a book, you can also listen to what the television is saying. It's possible to use your senses of sight and hearing simultaneously in this way, and there are other possible ways of using your ears, too. In this way, I recommend making full use of your sense of hearing.

To our surprise, more people than we would expect don't realize that their sense of hearing is a tool they can use and that by making good use of it, they can become capable in their work. The truth is that it's essential to use our ability to hear, and our sense of hearing can be used for further learning. A very large part of the information we learn in classrooms is acquired through our sense of hearing. In fact, the information we acquire through listening has a higher retention rate than information we acquire through our sense of sight. Spoken things that we listen to remain in our memory more easily than the written materials we read. Now is a time when television is at its height, and people nowadays watch a lot of television, because watching is easier than reading books or newspapers. However, when we look at the intellectual impact and compare the impact of watching television with the impact of reading, we see that one hour of television gives us the equivalent of only ten minutes of reading. Very well-developed television shows may sometimes contain a large quantity of information, but the content you get through television shows is typically very sparse. I feel that one hour of television will, on average, give you what ten minutes of reading will give you in terms of intellectual value.

Television shows are relatively easy to produce. A show can be created just by filming someone speaking. But you cannot write a book in the same way. To publish a book, someone needs to write a manuscript. Materials need to be gathered, and a lot of hard work is put into typing up each word to fill up the page. Proofreading is also required. In this sense, when I compare the quality of information you can obtain through television and printed materials, I would say that one hour of television equals only about ten minutes of reading.

Of course, in some cases, there is knowledge that's not obtainable through reading that can be gained through television. Television programs about international topics are one example. In some instances, it's easier to understand new subjects and topics and gain a sense of the worlds outside your areas of experience by watching television. Usually, we don't learn much about areas that we're less interested in or involved in, and we don't normally think about reading books about them either. For example, it's very rare to find someone in the dental profession who becomes determined to acquire and read books on distant-water fishing. However, you can get a sense of how distant-water fishing works by watching a documentary that shows fishing fleets catching tuna off the African coast of the Cape of Good Hope.

In this way, you can easily acquire information about unfamiliar subjects through the television. The quality of information you can learn from television about topics you don't have experience with is relatively high, in this way. But generally speaking, my advice is to bear in mind that the information from one hour of television will give you only ten minutes of reading. To put it another way, this means that the intellectual learning that six hours of television a day will give you is only as much as you can gain from one hour of daily reading. I heard that Americans watch five to seven hours of television and videos per day. But the amount of information or intellectual stimulation those seven hours of television give them is worth only a little over an hour of reading. And too much television could exhaust your eyes and mind, as well.

Thinking—Thinking Deeply to Advance Your Work Capability

Thinking is another important tool for self-development. To get better at your work, the task of thinking is essential. When you read, write, and listen, there are of course the parts of you that are reading, writing, and listening, but there's another part of you that's thinking. So, to advance your work capability, training yourself to think is essential.

Just as you can strengthen your muscles through training, you can strengthen your thinking ability further by training it. Those without a lot of thinking ability aren't able to think deeply on a subject for more than five minutes without getting distracted. Some people can't stay focused for more than a minute, or even ten seconds. When this type of person attempts to think about one topic, they get distracted and start to think about what they're having for dinner that night or other completely unrelated subjects. In this way, they're unable to put their ideas in order.

People who get distracted easily when they are thinking about something need to begin by training themselves to read, write, and listen. If they train themselves in this way, they'll notice their mind getting less distracted. It's essential to begin with this training and then use that as a basis to develop the ability to think.

People in higher positions will need to think deeply and think things through on many levels, so their thinking ability develops to high levels. Such people's work is very valuable.

If a superior were to ask, "Could you tell me your progress on this?" most people would respond, "I'll look into it again by tomorrow," and then report back the next day on one related point. If the superior then asks, "What if it were this way instead?" the subordinate would be unprepared with an answer and would respond, "I'll report to you on that tomorrow" and would report back the next day. The next day, the same thing would happen again, and he or she would report back the following day. At that rate, the person would need many days to complete one job.

When reporting your conclusion about something, you need to have three to five other ideas prepared in your mind. Even if you plan to give your superior conclusion A, you also need to consider and think through Idea B, Idea C, Idea D, and Idea E to conclude that choosing Idea A is best and report that to your superior. By being prepared in this way, you'll be able to answer your superior's questions immediately by explaining, "Concerning that, I also gave Idea B some consideration, but it would involve difficult issues. Idea C would be one way to solve those issues. But going with Idea C would lead to such-and-such results." This will help your superior understand the reason Idea A is best, and that will allow him or her to finish that job immediately. If you don't prepare in this way, you could be extending a job that could be finished in one day into three days and cause additional tasks to arise, and you'd be busy every day. So, it's important to think about what other ideas and possibilities there could be, even if you come to one conclusion.

The secretarial and strategic planning departments of a company especially demand this type of ability. It's necessary to have a high level of this ability in these departments. For example, managing the CEO's schedule is one of the jobs of the CEO's assistant. Many unexpected things can happen daily, such as unexpected appointments and incoming calls. It's hard to know what will happen, so the assistant will outline a general schedule, but a schedule written a week ago would not be of much use. It would cause tremendous trouble to the CEO if the assistant were to refuse to make any changes to the schedule. Suppose the CEO of one of your biggest client companies was to ask for a meeting. If the assistant were to ask his or her CEO to strictly follow the original schedule and not meet the customer, it would ruin the CEO's productivity. Even if there is a set schedule, the assistant needs to be able to immediately adjust it when higher-priority matters come up.

To avoid falling into a panic during these times, you also need to have Plan B, Plan C, and Plan D ready when you draft the original schedule. This is an ability that is necessary for a secretarial department. This is also an essential ability in sales and product development departments that work on developing new things. Ideas for product development often get turned down again and again, so you need to have a number of different ideas prepared so that when your best idea isn't accepted, you won't be left with nothing to do afterward.

This is the area of your hidden effort. Hidden effort is like ducks' wading feet. Ducks seem to glide on the water, but under the surface their feet are paddling furiously. This is the kind of effort that's essential to product development. People who don't spare any effort in this way become capable in their work, in the end. People who make this kind of effort all the time can respond to questions immediately and can also think flexibly. People who cannot respond in this way are, generally speaking, not thinking things through, so they have to rush to come up with an answer and can't immediately offer one.

3

The Importance of
Idea Planning Ability

Now Is an Age of Idea Planning Ability

Thirdly, I would also like to talk about the importance of idea planning ability as a tool for stepping up your work capability. Your set daily tasks are called routine work. This work requires an average level of ability. For instance, assembling products on a conveyor belt or putting together the different parts of a product in the right order is this type of job. In this type of job, someone else can take your place as a substitute for the day. There isn't a lot of creative, added value in this type of job. Work that generates significant added value is difficult to find a replacement person for, and one example of this type of work is planning ideas. In principle, planning ideas requires creating something new out of nothing. For example, if someone looks at the African savannah and only thinks, "There are wild animals running around this land," that would have no result. But someone else seeing the same land may think, "If I dig a well in this spot, it would create a source of water. Then I could raise livestock on this land. Later on, I could build a factory to manufacture products that I could sell internationally, and that would create commerce and help this country develop."

In this way, planning ideas has extremely high added value. In practice, when you actually plan ideas, it isn't about creating something from nothing. The materials already exist. It involves not just using those materials as they are, but looking at things in a new way, combining different materials, and creating something completely new. This leads to the ability to plan ideas, which enables you to create something unique.

The ability to look at things in new ways is extremely important. For example, to make walking outside with bare feet easier, we could try to pave the entire world with asphalt sidewalks. This would be an enormous endeavor requiring huge amounts of materials. It would not be an easy task to accomplish. But if we approached this project from a different perspective, we might think of producing shoes instead of paving sidewalks. With shoes, we can walk down any rocky road easily. This is one way of looking at things in a new way. Instead of saying you need to improve sidewalks, you can say that you need to protect people's feet. The person who invented shoes might have been thinking in this same way. There was probably someone who thought that by wearing shoes, people would be able to walk along rocky paths, sandy beaches, and even muddy roads. Many people who live in areas of the world where no one has come up with this idea are continuing to live barefoot even now.

Looking at things in a new way in this way leads to creating new things. It's important to have this ability to plan new ideas. People who have this ability have it innately but usually, they also gather a lot of information, which lets them come up with an abundance of different subjects and ideas. I mentioned the importance of reading and listening earlier on. People who don't have a large amount of information input are not capable of coming up with an abundance of new ideas. People with strong idea planning ability are constantly feeding their minds new information. Without it, they cannot come up with new ideas.

People who like to gather information are good at devising new ideas. New ideas don't suddenly pop up if you don't have any information. New ideas will come to you if you always keep an eye out for new information and gather it together to use. We are now in an age of idea planning. In this age of information and knowledge, we need to do more than just manufacture products. Planning new ideas is also important. We need to think about what needs to be accomplished and what's required to accomplish it. We're now in times when it's essential to do that and come up with new ideas so we can create new things.

The KJ Method for Writing Papers

I have just talked about the importance of gathering information to plan new ideas. Just gathering information isn't enough to create new products and new businesses, however. Here, I would like to explain various ways of developing your idea planning ability. First, the KJ Method is a famous one, named for the initials of its inventor, Mr. Jiro Kawakita (1920–2009). A cultural anthropologist who conducted frequent fieldwork, he developed this method to help him organize the variety of information he collected out in the field so he could write his research paper.

It's a method frequently used, nowadays, to write papers. Many people face difficulty finishing their papers on time because they have trouble putting together what they want to say. Even if students pray for a miracle from heaven to help them write 100 or 200 pages, it doesn't help much, and they can't come up with ideas to write about. Novelists also have a difficult time writing their stories.

It's said that even in these cases, the KJ Method can help anyone easily write a paper. Let me explain how to use this method in more detail. As you go about your daily life doing many things, I'm sure sometimes a thought will suddenly enter your mind. The thought enters suddenly, so you never really know when it will come to you. Sometimes, it can be difficult to come up with ideas to write about when you're thinking about the topic. But an idea might come to mind at the most surprising moments, such as while you're watching a video, having a cup of coffee, or taking a walk outside. Or, you might come across a paragraph or a sentence in a book that inspires you with a useful idea. It's important to always have a notepad with you for times like this.

They sell official labels to write on if you're using the KJ Method, but you don't necessarily need to use these specifically. For example, you could get large Post-it notes and leave them everywhere around you so you can grab one as soon as you have an idea. Write it down in one line, and then stick the note onto your desk. If you think of another idea, again, grab a Post-it note and stick that one on your desk as well. Write the ideas you think of on Post-it notes one after another. Write them down one by one when they come to mind, and stick them onto something. Then, once you've accumulated a number of these Post-its, by rearranging their order, you'll be able to see a certain flow and structure for your paper. By using this method, you'll be able to write a report or essay relatively easily.

It's usually quite difficult to suddenly write a paper. So, first, you would gather materials and read an appropriate number of books while writing notes on an index card. After you accumulate many of these index cards, you can lay them down and gather related topics into groups. By working in this way, you'll create several groups of cards that can be designated as chapter one, chapter two, chapter three, and so on, to create the overall structure of your manuscript to give you enough content to publish a book.

Even if your main ideas don't come to mind like a revelation from beginning to end, it's still possible to write a paper using this kind of process. In fact, the lecture this chapter is based on, "One Step Up in Your Work Capability," was developed using a variation of the KJ Method. On a sheet of paper, I wrote down notes for the lecture's main ideas: 1. Devote your life to your divine calling; 2. Self-development, reading, writing, listening, and thinking; 3. The importance of idea planning ability; and 4. Making full use of the power of teamwork. It took me only three minutes to write down these main ideas. To come up with them, I began by thinking of the title, "One Step Up in Your Work Capability." Then I pondered the content of this theme and I thought of, "Devote Your Life to Your Divine Calling," so I wrote this one sentence down on an index card. Then I also thought of the topic, "Self-development is essential," so I wrote this down. When I thought to myself about what is required for self-development, I thought of "reading, writing, listening, and thinking." Then, when I thought about what else is necessary, I also thought of the ability to create new ideas and the power of teamwork. When I arranged these ideas that came to mind separately into a certain order, I was able to finish creating a general outline for this lecture.

The amount of time this required of me was three minutes. (But this method isn't used for other chapters.) It might not usually work as quickly for other people, but if you created tens of those cards with more detailed topics, I'm sure you'd be able to use them to write an excellent paper. This KJ Method can be used to develop a general outline for huge college papers as well as for a short talk you might be giving. The human mind is apt to think of various ideas separately, so by writing them down, structurally rearranging them to flow, you'll be able to determine the contents of your paper. This is a very simple method that anyone can use, and it's one of the ways to enhance your idea planning ability.

The Brainstorming Method for New, Unique Ideas

Another way of enhancing your idea planning ability is the brainstorming method. "Brainstorming" sounds like there is a storm inside your mind. During corporate meetings, it's difficult to speak your mind freely, because there are usually people in higher positions in the room, such as executives, division managers, section managers, and so on. If one of your superiors were to say, "Why don't we try this idea?" all the people working under him or her would usually say, "Okay." Because of the power structure inside companies, it's difficult to voice your opinions and come up with ideas freely.

The brainstorming method is a way of putting aside everyone's positions in the company so you can have a free discussion together. With brainstorming there is a rule that no one can criticize anyone else's idea, no matter what kind of idea it is. When you allow everyone the chance to voice their ideas, no matter what they are, and let them speak freely, it facilitates the generation and expression of new ideas and opinions.

You can never know who a good idea might come from. It could at times come from the new staff. With regard to coming up with good ideas, your position in the company doesn't matter so much. When you make everyone's position in the company too clear, first- and second-year employees will have difficulty voicing their opinions. So, if you let everyone express their ideas without any regard for people's positions, everyone will be able to come up with interesting opinions. Also, instead of choosing to meet in a formal type of setting, it's good to hold brainstorming meetings in places like coffee shops to help people speak more freely.

If you gather a variety of interesting ideas in this way and find among them one that you think might work, you could develop a new product and start a project on it. This happens a lot with brainstorming meetings.

Brainstorming is a method that is useful not only for company meetings but also for individuals. I use it often myself. For example, when new thoughts and ideas don't come to mind, I gather books and periodicals on a variety of subjects at random and read them one after another. When I read many things that have no relation to one another in this way, they get combined and come together as a good idea from a completely different angle.

There are cases like this when integrating opposite things gives you an idea for a completely different approach that helps you create something entirely new. When you read a variety of things that have no relation to one another, gradually your way of looking at things will change, and that will help you have good ideas. The Japanese physicist Hideki Yukawa (1907–1981) is said to have spent time during his childhood doing his best to read classical Chinese texts out loud. Classical Chinese texts might not seem to directly relate to physics, but when he cultivated himself in this way, what he learned became useful in his later research. The philosophy of Chuang-tzu is said to have especially influenced his development of the elementary particle theory. Chuang-tzu's philosophy isn't associated at all with the study of physics, but by knowing this in your mind, you'll get inspiration in unexpected ways during your physics research. Suddenly, an idea that no other physicist would have thought of might come into your mind.

When you find yourself in a rut, combining completely different things enables you to see things from a different perspective or come up with new ideas. When you read and listen to completely unrelated things and blend them together, something completely new is created from them, just as oxygen and hydrogen molecules synthesize to produce water. I have just spoken about the importance of idea planning ability, and I hope you will cherish this ability.

There is great added value in the work of idea planning that's far more valuable than routine administrative work. I think that from now on, we will be living in an age marked by the power of idea planning ability.

4

Making Full Use of the Power of Teamwork

Idea Planning Based Purely on Winning Personal Recognition Tends to Fail

Now I would like to talk about the fourth way of stepping up your work capability, which is making full use of the power of teamwork. People seeking self-realization and seeking to make full use of themselves have very strong feelings about winning recognition from others. These feelings themselves are very valuable to have, but as you work hard with these feelings, you may find yourself the only one who is making use of your ability. It's not unusual for people to find themselves in this situation. There are times when you are putting forth a lot of effort, but the effect of your effort has reversed, meaning that the more effort you put into your work, the more the people around you are troubled by it.

You may wonder why people aren't giving you any recognition when you are developing yourself and putting in so much effort. In such cases, I think that you're missing the perspective of other people. You might be thinking only about yourself. When you submit new ideas, people who are thinking of getting more recognition for themselves, of getting praised for being clever enough to think of a good idea, aren't coming up with quality ideas. Even if you come up with a variety of new ideas, often the people around you might only feel troubled by them.

Nowadays, email is becoming more popular in companies. So, rather than using Japan's traditional approval system by circulating documents, many Japanese companies are now sending emails to people directly. It's possible for the lowest-level employees to send emails directly to the CEO. If that's allowed for any kind of opinion from anyone, the CEO could find 500 emails in his inbox, which could cause a huge issue, so they would have to be narrowed down in some way. Or, some employees may use email to communicate about where to have lunch together, which might not be an appropriate way to use email during work hours.

Think of Ideas that Also Benefit the Team as a Whole

If you're only thinking of giving your own opinions, it could end up inviting a lot of confusion. It's important to consider the other person's standpoint before expressing your opinion. For example, think about whether your ideas would be useful to him or her. When you do, you'll naturally develop your ideas further. Of the

500 emails that the CEO might receive, the content of over 490 of them would end up only wasting the CEO's time.

What's important is not to say that you thought of an idea. What's important is to consider how useful your idea would be to other people. Ideas that are submitted based on only thinking about yourself in the hope of recognition or praise often won't succeed. But if you are submitting your ideas in the hope that your superior will succeed and get an advancement through using your idea, then your idea has a strong possibility of being accepted.

Ideas that are based on the consideration of other people's perspective will often be successful ideas. But if raising your personal score by one point will result in other people's scores decreasing by one point, the total combined score of everyone will decrease. It's important to make efforts to raise your own score, but you need to always consider whether your ideas will also benefit your section, division, or company as a whole. If you're not thinking in this direction and instead are trying to increase your personal score only, the people around you will dislike that. If your idea would not benefit everyone as a whole in the end, then it's not a good idea.

In addition to that, if your self-development will cause trouble for others, it's not a good way of developing yourself. It's important to polish yourself, but in addition to that, think also about leveling up the power of everyone as a whole, and think about how to lead your entire team to success. Don't think only about your personal advancement; think also about ways of advancing that will also lead to the success of the people around you. It's important to always have this way of thinking inside you. If you're always thinking in this way, you will definitely step up your work capability.

CHAPTER THREE

THE FOUR PRINCIPLES OF HUMAN HAPPINESS

Overcoming Suffering through Love, Wisdom, Self-Reflection, and Progress

1

Four Ways to Get Out of Your Suffering

In this chapter, I would like to talk about the four principles of human happiness which I teach in Happy Science as "the principles of happiness." Many other teachings and theoretical ideas have stemmed from this set of principles, so, unfortunately, I won't be able to cover them all in this chapter. Here, I would like to discuss the topics which newcomers would easily understand and that would be useful talking points in the missionary work of Happy Science members already with an in-depth knowledge of the Truths.

These four principles didn't come to my mind one day just suddenly. They grew from my own real-life experiences. In this sense, it is true that they're the four principles to happiness. But they are also the fourfold path to enlightenment. And you could say, also, that this fourfold path to enlightenment is the four ways of getting out of human suffering and worries. So, in this chapter, I would like to discuss some common topics on the subject of human suffering and worries.

2

The Principle of Love—
Overcoming the Pain of Taking Love from Others

The Suffering of Feeling Unrecognized

The first topic I would like to talk about is on how to overcome the pain arising from taking love from others. When you look at human suffering in this world, most of the time it's the suffering of not getting the things you crave. What could this suffering of not getting the things you crave be, essentially? It's the pain inside of you that feels unloved and unrecognized by others.

There is the kind of recognition we receive from people's hearts and there is the kind of recognition which is material. Some kinds of recognition from the heart are people's kind words, thoughts, and treatment of you. There are also worldly fame and worldly status. The material forms of recognition would include financial wealth, cars, and houses. But many of them come from other people, in the end—they're not attained completely on your own. So, concentrating too strongly on getting them will sometimes bring suffering. When I look at modern people's suffering in this way, it's largely the suffering of not getting what they crave from others. You may suffer, for example, from not receiving a better salary, not getting promoted more quickly, and not getting more appreciation from your family, despite your earnest efforts. You may also suffer from not as many women liking you as you would wish, even though you've been working on improving your intelligence. Or you may suffer from not getting to work up to your true potential at work despite your great efforts.

In the end, the root of human suffering is the sense of unfulfillment inside people, the sense of frustration arising from not getting the things that they crave. It's the feeling in them that says, "I'm receiving poor treatment and being poorly appreciated, despite my efforts."

It's not such a difficult feeling to overcome when the recognition you crave is of a material kind. But it's difficult to overcome it when you crave to be appreciated from within someone's heart, especially someone you have a relationship with. This is because other people's hearts are beyond your control. Things don't go perfectly as you wish, so the person you crave to be loved or recognized by doesn't love you back, and the person you're not feeling drawn to is apt to feel attracted to you. This is the way things are apt to go in this world. Things don't seem to turn out the way we would like them to.

You Could Be Carrying Childhood Feelings of Frustration toward Your Parents into Adulthood

A lot of times, wanting to be loved in your human relationships, both the ones between men and women and other types, can feel like a thirsty and obsessive suffering, a suffering that Buddhist teachings fundamentally deny. It's the suffering of craving to get this or that from someone else, whether it's your significant other, your parents, or your children. For example, a child might yearn for his parents to be more capable. Or an adult pondering the cause of her present suffering might attribute it to her parents' poor working skills. Others might find the cause of their suffering in their parents' financial hardships, their parents not having been promoted to important positions, or their parents having come from the rural countryside. Still others might see the cause in their parents' advanced age, proneness to illness, divorce, or their parents living separately, being a single or widowed parent, or having had an extramarital affair resulting in family strife. Having had these kinds of childhood experiences, people may have felt unfulfilled in their relationships with their parents, and this childhood feeling of unfulfillment has persisted into adulthood and remains with them as the root of their current suffering.

They wish this sense of unfulfillment could be filled somehow, but it's difficult. For instance, you may wish that your parents had raised you differently during the first twenty years of your life.

But by the time you were 20, who your parents were as people was already fixed. Their way of being was already fixed solidly, and so was the course of their lives. At that stage in life—the stage of raising children—your parents' lives could no longer be changed. The parents, too, wish that they could start their lives over again, but they know that their lives have already become unchangeable. So, all they can say to you now is, "You were unlucky to have been born to us." Now, you're a full-grown adult and your parents no longer have the power to change your childhood. This is why your feelings of dissatisfaction rarely get resolved, no matter how much you want them to.

Then, when you are out in the real world, your childhood frustration can take on another shape. The fulfillment you originally sought from your parents now shifts to seeking it from your superiors and those above you. They could be the manager above you at work, the executives, or the CEO; you crave the recognition from them that you originally sought from your parents. But since you've only changed the person from whom you are seeking approval, it usually results in the same outcome. You will get the same results from your superiors as you did from your parents; you won't get the fulfillment you seek.

This is something that should not surprise you. Because your workplace has multiple employees, your superiors are supervising anywhere from several to tens to hundreds or even many more people. Whether they're a section manager, a division manager, or the CEO, they're supporting the livelihoods of many people. Like parents with many children who wish to treat them all fairly and avoid appearing to like or dislike some more than others, your superiors at work are also careful to avoid weakening everyone's morale.

For this reason, your wish for their exclusive favor won't be fulfilled nine times out of ten. It usually doesn't happen that way. A superior would rarely favor one particular person and raise his or her position. It could occur once in a while, but it's prone to lead to jealousy and badmouthing from the surrounding people, which would result in a setback. Usually, one person getting highly recognized leads to others speaking ill of this person and criticizing behind his or her back. This can become so difficult to endure that you might end up feeling like you'd be much better off not getting your superior's recognition. As a result, you will have to abandon your wish to be recognized by your superior in your parents' place, and you'll feel even more frustrated. There are cases like this, in which the person doesn't receive recognition from society.

In this way, the wish to be recognized in society has a strong relationship with the paternal principle. People who are frustrated by not receiving the recognition of their father as children are apt to seek the recognition of their superiors or someone in a similar position. This unfulfilled desire to be recognized by their father shifts to a desire to be recognized by society. But this usually doesn't work out as you wish it would. What happens next is you seek the kind of recognition you sought from your mother during your childhood years. If your father didn't give you recognition, there was still the hope for salvation from the unending love of your mother. You could feel fulfilled enough, thanks to her. In this way, even if you don't earn a promotion in the real world, you will still feel hope if you received your mother's love plentifully. In that case, you'll look for happiness within the home. There are very many cases of such people who look for another form of happiness from their family.

Then there are also cases when there wasn't enough of the mother's love, either. When you're a parent with more than one child, you can't avoid dividing your love among your two or three children. If you were to show favoritism toward one of them, the other children would feel that they were being treated unfairly. So, there are many people who, as children, had fathers who were very distant, and some people didn't receive much of their mothers' love, either. So, inside them is a feeling that says, "I wish my mother had loved me much more. She didn't play with me enough, praise me enough, or show me enough affection." People who have had these feelings are apt to feel frustrated in their home lives as adults, too.

Men who received enough of their mother's love as children are apt to seek warm and loving women to marry, and when they face setbacks in society, such a wife would be at their side to soothe

and console their wounded hearts. On the other hand, men with
not enough maternal love in their childhood home often cannot
find a loving person to marry, even if, deep down, they wish to do
so. Instead of someone kind, they're attracted to harsh and biting
women who could hurt their feelings. For some reason, they feel
drawn to the opposite kind of person. In such cases, they might get
hurt because the woman turns them down, or they might succeed
in marrying her but then live through a lot of hurt in the marriage.
In this way, their childhood setbacks become repeated with their
families. They have the same experiences from their childhood in
their adulthood.

People Who Endlessly Take Love from Others

In this way, the painful experiences of your childhood reappear in a
different shape. And this results in creating an unhappy life, in the
end. At the root of this unhappy life is a feeling that says, "I had an
unhappy childhood. I was never given enough. So, I wish someone
could erase this empty feeling for me. Would someone please fill
this emptiness inside me?"

People with these feelings inside them are like an unending
pit. However much love you give them, it vanishes into the pit.
Even if they're recognized for their work, it's not enough for

them. They continually seek more without end, thinking, "I want more and more recognition. I want more praise. I want to be promoted more quickly and be given a bigger salary. I also want to be awarded more in front of everyone." As a result of these feelings, people will stop recognizing them at one point or another. And when that time comes, they'll feel very unhappy and unfulfilled.

It is the same with them in their home. However much their wives or husbands love and take care of them, they never feel fulfilled, as if they have a bottomless swamp inside them. There is never satisfaction. However hard their spouse tries, they don't give their spouse recognition. They say, instead, "This isn't enough, and that's not enough, either." Nothing is ever enough for them. Their spouse could give them 99 percent. But they focus on the 1 percent that's not there and criticize them, saying, "This is what's not good enough in you. This is the side of you that isn't good enough," or "That's what's wrong about you."

If you are a husband, however hard you work in the competitive world of society to get promoted more quickly than your colleagues, there are wives who look only, for example, at your coming home late and are continually upset with you. But it's not that they'd be happy if you came home at a normal hour. There's no doubt they would feel angry at your slow advancement at work. This type of wife would blame you for things like slow promotions and little overtime pay. It's in the nature of this kind of spouse to criticize some part of you, and even if you improve on that aspect of yourself, these spouses will find another part of you to criticize. They're very difficult to satisfy, in this way.

Does it sound like I'm describing you? No matter what gender you are, upon reflection, you'll see that you are not 100 percent perfect yourself. So, you have to ask yourself, "Am I a perfect human being? Am I 100 percent perfect as a person? Do I have any right to seek perfection from another person? What would a perfect human being be like? Does such a thing as a perfect human being exist in reality?"

For instance, if you were to marry a famous female television celebrity, I think you'd have a difficult time finding happiness. It would be close to impossible for you to find true fulfillment. It would only turn into a source of suffering. She wouldn't be able to stay home, and her foremost interest would be getting onto television shows. She'd be too busy to think about you and take care of you. Her main focus would be wanting to be loved by all the men of the world, so you wouldn't necessarily find happiness by marrying a television celebrity (although there are some exceptions). The same could be said about marrying someone who's adored by all the women in the world. It would be very difficult to find happiness if you married a widely adored man. His behavior would concern you on a day-to-day basis.

There are cases like these. It's crucial to realize that you're not a 100 percent perfect human being yourself. And for this reason, you cannot continue to expect perfection from others to be able to accept them. You cannot keep saying that since you're a perfectionist, you won't be happy unless Mr. or Ms. Perfect comes into your life. By saying such things, you are effectively forever abandoning your own right to find happiness.

In this way, people who tend to continually take love from others often don't realize it, no matter how much the people around them pour their love into them. Instead of recognizing this love they're receiving, their attention goes to what's not enough. And because it's never enough, the people who are pouring their love into them become exhausted.

Having Gratitude for What You've Been Given

What's important, then, is to abandon thinking that you'll become happy by receiving from others. Your craving will see no end unless you throw this thought away. You could crave material things—material objects, wealth, the recognition of society, worldly fame, or good health—it doesn't matter what it is; the craving will never end. "The best" or "perfection" doesn't ever exist, in reality. In most cases, your suffering is being created by you.

You must put an end to this tendency of mind within yourself. Perhaps when you look at someone, you see the 1 percent that is missing. Perhaps it's 10 percent. But rather than working hard to blame this person for this 10 percent, why not look at the 90 percent this person has accomplished? If you crave 100 percent from your wife, it's very normal for there to be disharmony in your home. Some wives may make the effort to fulfill that expectation if you request it. But a person of that type would probably be prone to psychosomatic disorders. Or a father-in-law or a mother-in-law might expect 100 percent from the wife, so the wife does her best, but she will probably fall into depression eventually as a result. This is why it's important to stop asking others to give you 100 percent, and instead, draw your attention to what they are accomplishing well.

By a mystery, when you make this shift, the world will start to change around you. Stop the mental pattern of seeking from others, wanting to gain something from others, wanting to receive from others, and wanting to be given things by others to be happy, and instead begin to discover what you've been given already. Or, for example, stop looking at the wrong aspects in other people and instead look at their good sides. When you do, this change in your recognition of them and your way of thinking about them will become a way of giving something to them from within yourself.

In this world, there are wives who make an effort to give 90 percent but are criticized for the 10 percent they don't fulfill.

There are also wives who tell their husbands, "You're a great person. I just can't stand this habit of yours." The wife may say, "You are a really great guy, but I just don't like all the hair wax you put in your hair." "I wish you'd shave your beard." "The way your eye is slanted upward at the end bothers me a lot." "You snort sometimes." "You grind your teeth at night." There are various cases like these.

If you are saying to others, "I just can't stand this one thing," this is saying that you want to be unhappy. In other words, people who say this about others actually want a reason to be unhappy. If you are like them, you are trying to find something to blame your unhappiness on.

If you want to be happy instead, you have to recognize other people's good sides. Be very grateful for what they give you, and decide to stop craving things from other people. Tell yourself that now it's time to stop thinking this way; now it's time to look at what others have been giving you. And from now on, think about being on the side of giving and repaying instead of taking and receiving.

For example, the husband might always come home late from work, but there must be some reason for it. So, as his wife, you could give him words of appreciation for working so hard at his job. Something this simple could make a huge difference. If he knows that whatever explanation he gives you for coming home late will be of no use, then all he'll say to you is, "I need dinner," "I'm going to

THE FOUR PRINCIPLES OF HUMAN HAPPINESS

take a bath," and "I'm going to bed." But if you could give him some words of appreciation, he might sometimes suddenly open his heart to you.

It Doesn't Cost a Penny to Improve Human Relationships

First, it's essential to realize that no one can become happy by looking at what's lacking in others and expecting them to fix it. They've already given you many things. When you begin by having gratitude for them, you will seek to repay them, and you will want to live a life of giving back to others. The truth is that in a life of giving back, the path to unhappiness doesn't exist. When you enter a life of repaying others, there cannot be any unhappiness for you.

It's not possible to repay others 100 percent. But if you could give them back even 1 percent, it would make you happier by 1 percent. If you could return 10 percent to others, it will make you 10 percent happier. If you can raise this to 50 percent, it will make you 50 percent happier, and if you can repay as much as 90 percent to others, you will gain 90 percent more happiness inside yourself. For this reason, if you shift your thinking toward loving and repaying others, the unhappiness in your life will ultimately vanish. This is the way we create happiness.

For this reason, no one is happier than the one who sees others' happiness as their own. People who enjoy it when other people are *un*happy won't find true happiness. But people who feel happy when they see other people's lives getting better—these are the very people in possession of the happiness mentality.

In most cases, the suffering of trying to take love from others revolves around the dissatisfied and frustrated feelings you get from your human relationships. It's the feeling of dissatisfaction that comes from the thought, "No one is giving me anything." But however much you seek things from others, you must realize that this attitude is only further paving your path down the antlion's pit. You have to abandon this way of thinking and feel grateful for the recognition you've been given. And instead of seeking to get something from other people, think about what you have neglected to do for others.

For example, you might have long-held feelings of anger toward your superior for not recognizing you. Think about whether you have done something to support your superior during the time you've had these feelings. Have you tried to help him or her become more recognized and receive advancements in the company? You probably haven't. But even though you haven't done this for your superior, maybe you can't stop thinking about the recognition he or she hasn't given you. Ask yourself, "Have I tried to support my superior's advancement at work? Have I worked very hard to do that and to cooperate with my superior?" You might be under the assumption that you have, but from your superior's standpoint, it's not the case.

Your superior may be thinking, "This guy works very hard during the month before bonuses are given out. But once he gets his bonus, he's prone to going back to working less again." This is often the case.

In your own mind, you might be under the impression that you've been working hard. But from the other person's standpoint, you might seem to be quite an egoist who works hard only when you stand to benefit from it and won't do any work beyond that. But you don't realize this, so you think to yourself, "I worked very hard at this, but I haven't received any recognition for my work." What you must do, then, is look at yourself from the other person's standpoint, and instead of looking at what you haven't gotten from others, look at what you, yourself, haven't given to others. Look at this aspect, instead, and self-reflect deeply on this point, and then take action. This is the real path to happiness.

Some people have never given their spouse a single compliment, even after many years of being together and many years of their spouse working hard for them. Why do they hesitate? It doesn't even cost a penny to pay a compliment. For example, if your wife put on especially beautiful makeup today and looks more beautiful than usual, all you have to do is compliment her on how beautiful she looks. Or if your husband came home from work 10 minutes earlier than usual today, compliment him. Even if it's just 10 minutes earlier than normal, just by saying to him, "You came home earlier than usual today. You must have worked very hard today," you'll make him feel happy, and he'll think to himself, "It makes her happy when I plan my work efficiently and succeed in coming home early." Even saying something that simple is a nice thing to do.

There are also people who assert themselves a lot, saying, "Me, me." But asserting themselves doesn't lead many of them to success. There are indeed some people who become successful by acting that way, but they usually end up tripping themselves up at one point or another down the road. They normally come to a point when they stumble.

So, what's important is to be humble. It doesn't cost you a penny to do so. Be polite toward others. It's very important to make continuous efforts. Otherwise, you could trip up and stumble when you assert yourself too much.

In this way, it doesn't cost you a penny to improve your human relationships. No money at all is required to do this. All that's needed is to change your attitude and say something. It might require the use of a little bit of your energy, maybe one Calorie's worth of physical energy. But that's almost nothing to speak of.

Being human, people are apt to remember for a very long time about the things people say to them—for many decades. So, they will also remember the praise they've received. If they're criticized, they'll remember it for a decade, and the same holds true if they're praised. They might feel as if they've been praised continually for 10 years. In reality, they were praised at just one moment in time, but that one moment makes a big difference.

Not one cent is required to improve your human relationships and steer them toward happiness. There is no sweat or toil required of you. Instead, what's essential is to change your attitude of mind and show others your goodwill in a concrete way, no matter how small. I feel that this is so important.

When you look at human suffering in this world, most of it is the pain of trying to take love from someone else. It's suffering from the feeling, "I want more, I want more." So, you must stop wanting to get something more and instead think of what you can do for others. Your worries will vanish when you do. This is also an aspect of enlightenment that can change your perspective. This connects with my discussion of the principle of love and its most fundamental aspects.

3

The Principle of Wisdom—
Stop Lamenting Not Being Smart Enough and Study

Almost Everyone Worries about Whether They're Smart Enough

Second, I would like to discuss the topic, "Stop lamenting not being smart enough and study." This topic relates to the principle of wisdom.

My discussion would go on endlessly if I were to take a difficult approach to this topic. So, I would like to talk about something simple. For people who say, "I'm unhappy. I'm miserable because I'm not given love from others," their path to happiness is the principle of love. To them, happiness is found through giving love to others, and that's what I have just explained.

Then there are people who lament that they aren't intelligent enough. Many people in the world think this is only true of themselves, and if you look at everyone, 99.9999999 percent of people are worrying that they're not as intelligent as others. It's a mystery, and since you cannot peek into other people's minds, you're apt to think that you're the only person who worries about this. But it's actually a worry that many people have about themselves.

For example, sometimes people look only at another person's academic background. And when they look at other's college education, they notice when someone attended a top-flight university. But can we say that graduating from a top-flight university automatically means you're an intelligent person? Actually, not everyone who went to those universities thinks of themselves as intelligent and feels filled with pride and joy about it. In fact, people who've achieved a lot academically tend to feel a sense of inferiority easily. People who haven't studied as much and instead have had more fun in their lives, in truth, have fewer feelings of inferiority. And smarter people who studied as much as possible end up feeling a more severe sense of inferiority when they see gaps between themselves and others.

You may be thinking, "It must be nice to be a top-flight university graduate. She must never feel inferior. Since I attended a second-tier college, I'm filled with a sense of being inferior to others." But the truth is that, inside that competitive world, the feelings of inferiority that these top-flight university graduates confront during setbacks are far more severe. They feel a strong and severe feeling of inferiority. The difference between one or two points on their exam score could make them suffer hugely from the idea that the other person is a genius and their intelligence is only ordinary. To think in this way is unnecessary, though. It doesn't mean anything to those who don't find value in those things. But people who value them very highly react very sensitively to small differences. This is the reason why top-flight university graduates may feel a strong sense of inferiority. For this reason, it's not right to base your assessments of people on external factors such as how highly ranked their university is.

Academic Achievement Doesn't Necessarily Guarantee Success

Also, people with high grades among highly educated people are not necessarily happy. Even though they've achieved a lot academically, they create other worries for themselves; for example, they worry that they won't be promoted, will get a poor evaluation at work, or will fail to become wealthy despite their high academic achievements. These things are very worrisome to them.

These worries are universal. We can see a certain rule that the academically successful don't earn the most wealth. On the contrary, the not-so-studious people who also spent time enjoying their lives and accumulating life experiences are the ones who are apt to be the most successful at earning wealth after graduation. It's truly a mystery. For some reason, people who took it moderately easy in their academics and were involved in extracurricular activities, worked at part-time jobs, or traveled abroad, usually get promoted quickly, move around to different companies, and see steady increases in their income.

On the other hand, those who are academically very studious tend to become professors or public servants and earn incomes that stay at a modest level. For example, public servants' pay is sourced from citizens' taxes, so their salaries can't be very high. When their salaries become higher than the private sector's, it places a heavy tax burden on the people of their country. So, public servants' salaries are set with a basic premise of being lower than salaries in the private sector, and this low salary might become a cause of worry.

For example, you could be a University of Tokyo graduate. But even if you become a high-ranking public official, your pay will still be half the salary of someone employed by a private company during the last several decades. So, even though you were academically more exceptional, your salary comes out to half of other people's. (Of course, we are currently going through a downward economy in the private sector also.) It's much worse for university professors. If you ask them, they will tell you, "Since public servants' salaries are half of the private sector's salaries, they're still in better shape than we are. If you study even more than they do and become a university professor, you'll only make a third of what you could make in private businesses. I was studying diligently while the other students were having fun. That's how I went to graduate school. But my salary is still a third of theirs. It's really difficult."

They have feelings of complaint and dissatisfaction like that, but if you look closely at their work, you find that it's fair for them to receive lower salaries than people in the private sector. The reason is that they aren't doing much actual work. In their profession, doing well on examinations can help them get through their entire lives. But in the private sector, people are working and being evaluated on a day-to-day basis. This is like taking an exam every day, or an exam every month.

In academia, they say, "If you get accepted once, then you are guaranteed to keep your job for the rest of your life." It's much different in the private sector. People who work in jobs where they're being evaluated every day are going through severer things. Earning a high income is a difficult thing to do under this kind of daily testing and evaluation of your work. In comparison, it's very easy for you if passing an exam or finishing a dissertation will certify you for your job for the next decade. University professors in Japan, in this way, are guaranteed 10 years in their job without having to write a single essay.

A professor of mine once told me that he had only written one book in 17 years. If professors published the notes to their classroom lectures, they wouldn't be able to give those lectures in class anymore, so they wait till they retire to publish them. They can't show them to others, because if they did, they wouldn't be able to give the same lectures every year. If they published them, they would need to talk about new things. So, instead, they finally publish their classroom lectures at retirement, after having given the same lectures for 30 years. Frankly speaking, they're the lazy type of people, and it's only natural for their income not to increase. Compared to them, high earners are earnestly working every day. To make steady progress, they are thinking of and developing new things all the time.

This is why you can't necessarily say that you'll fail because you're not as intelligent as others or that you'll succeed because you are intelligent. The trend in these modern times has been to follow the academic pyramid, creating far more defeated people than winners, if we look purely at the number of people at each level. The difference is striking. Purely looking at the number of the academically defeated, including academic exam scores, 70 or 80 percent of people could be categorized as the defeated. If everyone who doesn't succeed in academia were unhappy, that would mean that there are great numbers of unhappy people. However, this, indeed, isn't the right way of judging people, actually. Succeeding academically or at examinations is, indeed, one stepping-stone. If you use academic success as a springboard, the further efforts you make will lead you down a path of success. But if instead, you decide to rest on your laurels, it will stop there, and you'll travel the route of not much success.

It is people who do the opposite, people who put hard work into their jobs, who will become successful down the line. This is why we shouldn't think of academic success or high academic ability as absolute, and it's also important to know that academically successful people are suffering in real life. I think that knowing this truth will ease your mind, even if you are one of the defeated.

The very studious people cannot understand why the people who spent time in college doing enjoyable things are receiving promotions and earning higher incomes. It's a complete mystery to them, and this feeling is the source of their suffering. It's because those people who spent time doing enjoyable things are required to demonstrate capabilities that never get tested on exams. They are recognized for demonstrating abilities that are not included in academic examinations. So, it cannot be helped.

Heaven works fairly in this sense. When heaven gives one kind of talent to someone, it usually doesn't give that person other kinds of talents. For this reason, if you don't have a certain kind of talent, you'll usually find your talent in another area. You never know just where your talent might be hidden, but we come into this world as various types of people, each with a talent of our own.

Your Intelligence Is Determined by Effort

We are apt to look at the intelligence we're born with as something fixed at birth. It's wrong to say that we haven't been born with anything inherent inside us. It is true that as babies, we are born with some higher or lower level of intelligence. There are some children who are naturally sharp, active, or slower from birth, and it's something we also recognize during children's elementary and middle school years. So, something inherent exists within us, it's true.

But at the conclusion of your life in this world, your life will receive an evaluation score. When you receive that score, what was innately within you before birth won't have any influence. What you will be graded on is what you have done in this life since the time you were born into this world. From different starting points, you and others set off on your lives. It's this distance—showing how far you have traveled from your starting point—that you will be evaluated on. It's how much you persevered from that point on that will determine your score for this life. It's important to look at your life from this perspective.

Your life since birth depends a lot on your efforts, and through the law of cause and effect, you will be evaluated on this aspect of the effort. In addition, the law of cause and effect is typically linked with studying. The effort you put into studying normally leads to getting better in your studies, the more effort you put toward it. I think it's possible to lament the innate talents you were born with. By around age 20, the evaluation of your various academic abilities is complete, for the most part, and it's possible to lament this first half or one-third of your life. It's a highly competitive world that we live in, to be straightforward, and if we look purely at those who are successful and those who are defeated, the number of the defeated are far greater. However, if you were to label yourself as a defeated person and stop there, your whole life would become a time of suffering and unhappiness. You have to realize this about your life.

If you only look at everyone's innate talents since birth, the starting lines will be different depending on the person. But in the end, your life's evaluation score will be determined by how much you have grown since then, how far you have traveled from that starting line, and how much hard work you have put into your journey of life. Whatever you did before that starting point may have impacted your past lives, but they don't have any influence on the life you are living now. Regarding this present life, you are going to be evaluated by how much effort you have made from that point on. This is one way that I would like you to think.

Another way you should think is that "even genius cannot surpass effort"—no one can win against people of effort. People who are known to be intelligent will become average within a year if they neglect their studies. It's the simple truth. It takes great effort for people to develop their intelligence, but it's actually extremely easy to stumble from that point on. So, your success in life is not the result of your intelligence at birth, and neither is it the result of fate.

Some children attend academically excellent prep schools, but after that, they may not be able to keep up in class, and some could become delinquent students in the end. They may become children who cause a lot of trouble for their parents. This isn't just an outcome of fate, nor a result of how intelligent or unintelligent the children are. It's not just about issues of that kind. It depends ultimately on the child's own values, feelings, and ways of thinking. Therefore, you shouldn't think of your intelligence as a matter of fate.

There are also different forms of intelligence. There is the academic kind of intelligence related to doing well in school, and there's also another worldly kind of intelligence. The intelligence you have in real life, in the end, depends on whether you know the principle of success. The principle of success is something we aren't taught in school. We're not taught about it in elementary school, middle school, high school, or college. Our academic education is one foundation of our lives, but the principle of success is something we have to learn through our own real-life experiences. And those who learn the principle of success will, in the end, become the people who are intelligent in the worldly sense.

If you cannot completely learn this principle, it will mean, regretfully, that you have loved your superficial achievements too much. It will mean that you chose to focus studying to get high grades on exams and, in the end, that you weren't able to completely learn the principles of this-worldly success.

It's Possible to Win the Battle against Yourself

Many people in this world lament that they're not as intelligent as they would like to be. To begin by giving you the answer, in the final analysis, it's not possible to succeed by comparing yourself with others. You cannot succeed if you compare yourself to other people, if you live inside a world of comparison. Instead, see your problems as something about yourself, and look at how much you've grown, saying, "When I was born, I was about this intelligent. But I studied hard, and now I'm capable of this much."

This is a fight against yourself, an absolute fight. It's a competition that all people are capable of winning. It's possible to succeed by saying to yourself, "When I compare myself now with how smart I was at the beginning of my life, in my elementary school, middle school, and high school years, I see that I've persevered and have come this far." It's always possible to win this fight against yourself.

If you remain in the world of competition against other people, it's difficult to succeed. At the same time, when you look at the later outcomes of people who did well in school, they often have not won the fight of life. There are people who are always very good at their studies, and you may wonder how they got along later in their life. You might find that some of them were employed by a certain government ministry but then committed suicide later on.

Maybe that government ministry hires about 20 people every year as elite government officials. But on average, 10 percent of these hires later commit suicide. Maybe the divorce rate is also unusually high in this group of people. From that standpoint, it's difficult to confidently say that they've been successful people. (In some rare cases, there are also idealistic types among them.)

The reason they take their own lives is, in the end, their overconfidence in their own capabilities. They imagine that they are capable of much more, but they can't perform at the level they imagined for themselves. They suffer through a lot of anguish of this kind. Or they may feel concerned that someone else will rise to the position of division director but they, themselves, won't go higher than a section manager. They may feel concerned that they'll become a division director, while someone else might get promoted to a vice minister position. They suffer from these thoughts, and they anguish over them so much that they choose to take their own lives. There are also others who do so because of issues with human relationships.

It's unnecessarily foolish to take your own life. It's a great shame to do such a thing. Inside a small world, they compete against others for superiority, and when they feel defeated, they choose death over life. I have to say that they are living in a world that is all too small. The world they are looking at is much too small, and this is the reason they resort to such a decision. They are looking at their successes and defeats based on the standards of a very limited world, and this is causing them to take this kind of action. Such outcomes can be a result of being very studious. So, it's better to think that you will not succeed through living in a world of competition with others, in the end. Fights, in the end, are fights with yourself.

It's good to be aware, to some extent, that you were born with a greater or lesser degree of intelligence. It would be a lie to say that no such differences exist. To some degree, this is a truth. But what you ought to do is find happiness from looking at the original evaluation points you were born with and see how much "interest" you've earned over the years since that time. If you can find happiness in how much your intelligence has grown since then, then there can be no mistakes, and there can be no defeats in your life.

Knowing Can Keep You from Stumbling

Academic ability is related to intelligence. But there is also another side of intelligence, as I explained earlier. Whether you know about the principle of success in this world also affects whether you will succeed or fail in life. This is an aspect of life that other people cannot teach you. How it should be applied to each person differs from person to person, and there is no one, not even a fortuneteller, who can teach you one thing at a time what will lead to failure and what will lead to success. If I were to tell you something simple and basic about it, it's that we human beings don't stumble over things we know about. Please remember this fact.

You won't stumble over things you know about. But there are so many things in life that you don't know about. You will encounter many things that are unknown to you, and you will think, "That's something other people have experienced, but I haven't," and "Older people know that about life, but it's the first time I've experienced something like this before."

Your success rate regarding things you do not know about is fifty-fifty. It's difficult to know whether you will succeed or fail at them. But if it's something you already know about, your chance of success rises from fifty-fifty to 100 percent—or if you can't succeed completely, you can succeed more than 90 percent. You will often succeed at things when you know that taking a particular kind of action will lead to a particular kind of result.

The same can be said of a chess player. Chess players will succeed if they know certain chess moves. Against another player who doesn't know those moves, your success rate will be perfect, but it would be more difficult to win a game against someone who knows them. We are like chess players. We don't stumble over things we already know about.

Most of the people of the world are amateurs when it comes to life experiences and life's successes and failures. It's very difficult to find someone who has studied these things thoroughly. If anyone were to study them completely, that person would never stumble in life. But usually, more than 90 percent of us are amateurs. This is the reason we all stumble when we're confronted by things that are new to us. This is why knowing is important.

So, what can you do to know more? First, you can gain knowledge by reading. This is one way. Of course, it's possible to gather knowledge from television, movies, novels, and other types of materials. You could also listen to people's stories. There are various paths to take. So, if you're feeling lost, the first step is to collect information that is needed to make the necessary decisions. I will repeat again that you will not see failure if you already have the relevant knowledge.

When you observe people who have been academically successful but have been unsuccessful in their lives, you see that most of them do not know enough about the evils of life. The curriculums set by the education ministry include nothing at all about life's evils. Just studying their set curriculum will not teach you about the evils, sufferings, setbacks, and illusions of life. For example, they will not teach you things like, "If you do these things, you are apt to stumble in life," and "There are people in the world who think in such-and-such a way, and they could cause you to stumble; they could lead you into a trap."

It would be easy if you were lucky and you could avoid facing that kind of danger. In that case, you could find a good route to follow to rise smoothly to success. But if that is not the case for you, you will eventually confront the evils of life. In this regard, people who are already aware of them are definitely in a stronger position.

So, it's important to have prior knowledge about what people usually do in different types of situations.

If it's regarding financial matters, for example, if you were a bank employee, you'd be required to know certain types of principles that say things like, "If you lend money to a certain type of person, it will result in a certain outcome." A number of patterns exist that will tell you, "This type of company is prone to going under because of this reason, that reason, and this reason," or, "There are some issues in the CEO's personal life. The issues are here, here, and here. Companies run by these types of people usually fail, eventually." By knowing these things, you would be able to avoid stumbling. But if you were to lend the bank's money to such types of people because you lacked this knowledge, the money could become irrecoverable, which would negatively impact your prospects for advancement in the company.

You are required to know about these various facets of life. It might not be possible to learn about them only by reading written materials. You will, after all, need to listen to other people's life experiences and real-life stories. It's important to learn about the evils of life in this way.

People who want to succeed at achieving good in this world will also need to know about evil. People who have the power to fight evil are also strong concerning the good. Evil can sometimes spread when people don't know about it. But by knowing about evil and being able to see through it, you will be able to prevent it from actualizing.

People who try to deceive you and lure you into a trap do exist in this world. But even if they don't have the intention to do so, it's part of being human that they would do such things when they're confronted with certain situations. Study these things deeply. By doing so, you will be able to avoid stumbling in your life and enter the path of happiness.

There are people like that who are evil, but it's also righteousness to prevent these types of people from committing those evils. It's a common occurrence to see good people who stumble in this way due to being deceived. In a world where evil is allowed to spread in this way, righteous people would fail to remain righteous. If we allowed evil to grow in this way, righteous people would become accessories to evil.

Therefore, hold a wide range of interests and closely observe the problems associated with the evils of life along with what causes people to fall, stumble, and make mistakes. There is a limit to your own experiences in this regard, so it's important that you carefully study the people around you, such as your friends, parents, brothers, sisters, relatives, and other acquaintances. There will definitely be things to learn from in their experiences. Watch carefully for the reasons people stumble, what causes them to take the path of evil, and what leads them to become involved in wrong things. By doing so, you will be able to learn many things about life. Those who know about evil will not stumble. And those who don't know about it will be defeated by the first blow. This happens in reality. The saying "knowledge is power" is also true in this respect. Please study this deeply.

I have said that you don't need to regret being less intelligent in the academic sense. In addition to that, I also want to say that people do not meet failure in areas of life they already know about, and in this sense, it's important to make an effort to learn about various things. In other words, if you have the time to wish that you were smarter, you should spend that time continually working to gather knowledge and study so you'll be able to make the right decisions. It's another path to becoming happier.

The management of an organization depends on its people and its CEO alone. Even within the same company, there are times when the company would go down if it were run by a particular person but wouldn't go down if the CEO were replaced. There are cases like this. And the CEOs who lead their companies to go under don't usually understand the reason that the company is going under. In their position, they push things forward without knowing the cause. And because these CEOs haven't studied enough from other people's experiences and knowledge, they lead their company to its downfall. This is the reason. In the final analysis, rather than regretting the things you were born with and what's already in your past, it's important to make proactive efforts and persevere to open the way forward.

4

The Principle of Self-Reflection—
Evil Spiritual Disturbances Can Be
Cut Off through Self-Reflection

More Than Half of Modern People Are
Experiencing Evil Spiritual Disturbances

Third, I would like to talk about cutting off evil spiritual disturbances through self-reflection. People who don't know about spiritual things don't realize this, but spiritual things are a reality. In this chapter, I began by saying that those who are suffering because they're trying to take love from others would become happier if they began giving love to others instead. Next, I said that rather than regretting being less intelligent than you might like, you should spend time studying and gaining knowledge and succeed in your life that way. This was referring to the principle of wisdom. Both of these are things you can do by yourself. So, these are the two paths I've shown you that will lead to happiness that begins with yourself. These are also the paths to enlightenment. Enlightenment begins with yourself: You set off on the path by starting with yourself.

The same can be said about self-reflection. One of the reasons you don't succeed in life and enter the path to defeat is actually a spiritual issue. In other words, you can also be influenced by evil spirits. People who did not believe in the existence of heaven and hell while they were living or if they believed in them, they believed in a wrong type of religion, have a difficult time finding heaven in the afterlife. When they can't go to heaven, they may fall to hell, but they may try to stay in this world in some way or another. People who can't enter heaven wish to stay in this world. They basically don't want to die.

To stay in this world, they can either possess the people in this world or possess certain places in this world. These are the only two possibilities. The spirits are attached to this third-dimensional, material world. And this attachment they have is preventing them from leaving this world. If you become possessed by these spirits, your life could possibly take a bad turn. It's possible that this may happen.

I don't want to speak too much about spirits and curses and cause people to feel afraid or frightened of them. But spiritual possession is an issue that exists in real life. I cannot show you the numbers and statistics to prove this to you in a clear way. But I would say that more than half of people, nowadays, are under the negative influence of evil spirits. I think that this is the reality of the state of this modern world. It's often the case that one or two evil spirits are exerting some kind of influence on a person.

Especially when the spirit and the consciousness of the living person become extremely similar, and they come to share the same kinds of values, life perspectives, and ways of behaving, it becomes difficult to tell which one is influencing the living person's actions. It becomes difficult to differentiate which being this person is. Sometimes, the living person will begin to show the same habits and behavior patterns as the non-living person, and he or she will confront the same path of destruction, in the end. It's almost scary how true this is.

For this reason, if you have a relative who followed a particular path of destruction and then died, you will need to be careful. Sometimes the possessed person will tread the same path. This is not a result of some sort of a connection; it's actually the result of the influence of a spirit who hasn't gone to heaven. So, in cases like these, you'll need to recognize that this influence is there.

Therefore, if there is something inside your mind that has the same vibrations as this sort of spirit, if you have this kind of tendency inside your mind, you have to make the effort to change this aspect of yourself. What could happen as a result of becoming possessed by an evil spirit is that your swaying emotions could get stronger. What's characteristic is to become very prone to rage and sudden bouts of anger. What also happens when you are possessed by an evil spirit is that you begin to see the world from an opposite perspective. Everything will look as if it's the other way around to you. For example, if you refer to what I've said about shifting your thinking from taking love from others to giving love to others, you won't find inside you any feelings of wishing to give love to others.

When you are possessed by an evil spirit, you are always suffering, believing you are being victimized, and you will feel dissatisfaction with other people and your environment. Your life perspective becomes the opposite of everything, and therefore, you will acquire a life perspective that says, "I just have to criticize people who are happy and are succeeding in life." And you *won't* have any feelings that say, "I'll make the effort to find the way myself," or "I'm going to do something for the sake of others." You will look at others and always see them as bad people, and you will keep recognizing their bad points.

Then, you'll gradually feel as though you are not yourself anymore. You'll recognize that you're being strongly influenced by another being, that your life is swinging greatly in another direction. Especially when you fall into a habit of not getting enough sleep or drinking to a point of intoxication, it will become difficult to remove the evil spirit from you.

Self-Reflection Is the Easiest Weapon to Use in the Fight against Evil Spirits

To avoid being possessed by evil spirits, it's extremely important to remain rational. When you are possessed by an evil spirit, your swaying emotions will become very pronounced. If you find yourself in such a situation, then get the necessary amount of sleep, be mindful to take care of your health, and try to improve your overall condition in this way.

Improving your condition is a must, but there is also a weapon you can use to fight evil spirits. The easiest weapon to use against them is the practice of self-reflection. Even if you are being possessed by an evil spirit, don't place too much blame on the evil spirit itself. If it's capable of possessing you, that means that there is definitely something inside you that is in tune with it and attracting it to you. Therefore, you have to think that it's not the evil spirit you are fighting against; you are fighting against the evil within your own mind.

You may have heard the story of Shakyamuni Buddha conquering the temptations of Devils and attaining enlightenment. When many Devils are surrounding and attacking you, it means that there is something inside you attracting them to you. When you're confronting a worry, like the very final temptation, a Devil is apt to try to sneak into your mind. When weak spots like this that Devils can sneak into vanish, they'll no longer be able to possess you, and they'll detach from you.

When evil spirits become attached to you, they do so in the exact same way that you plug a cord into an electric socket. They attach themselves to you like glue and magnify your feeling of exhaustion and the weight of your worries. It makes them extremely happy to see someone worrying and suffering, and they think to themselves, "I'm going to make this person suffer even more," "Let's drive this person to the limit, so he'll kill himself," and "I'm going to find a way to destroy this person's life." These are the types of thoughts that come to influence you.

For example, if you go to a spot that's famous for suicide, there are many spirits living in places like that. When people confronting similar worries as these spirits come to these locations, the evil spirits easily possess them, and they commit suicide in the same way that those spirits did. They become influenced by these earthbound spirits. For this reason, you should avoid going to places where people often die. I wouldn't recommend playing "dare" with others to go to these types of locations, and I advise everyone not to go near them.

In this way, you could become possessed by spirits that are attached to a certain location, or you could also become possessed by a spirit with whom you had a connection while he or she was alive. Spirits like that will come to you rather easily. But even spirits that don't have such a connection with you could become completely in tune with your mind's vibrations. Distance doesn't matter in the spiritual world, so they can come from anywhere and become connected to you.

Therefore, if you think that your mind could be in tune with hell, first start with things that you can do by yourself. Self-reflection will become your weapon of choice in doing so.

Evil Spirits Become Attracted to Your Attachments

This is a teaching that has been taught repeatedly in Buddhism, and it's that evil spirits sneak into your mind through your attachments. When you have an attachment to something, the root of this attachment in your mind is something this-worldly. It's the aspect of you that is attached to things in this world and is saying, "I want this. I want that," and this is creating your problem. This is usually the source of your attachment.

This means that if you can point out what your attachment is, you are near the path to freeing yourself of it. If you cannot recognize what your attachment could be, then reflect on the things you are thinking about throughout the day during the times you're not really consciously thinking. The thoughts inside your mind that occur repeatedly throughout the day, the thoughts that you think about all day long, are indicating what your attachment is. It's the thought that comes up again and again throughout your days, and you sometimes happen to realize you were thinking about it. It's these thoughts that are taking up a lot of the room within your mind.

For example, it could be thoughts about your past. When you realize it, you are thinking about the experience of being abused by your father during your childhood years. Or you suddenly realize that you're constantly thinking about the girlfriend you broke up with years ago or about the superior you had a falling out with a very long time ago. Or you could be thinking about your child all the time.

If you have thoughts that you're not consciously thinking about—that you're thinking about without realizing it—and your mind returns to them all the time, these are your attachments, especially if you return to them not just seldomly or just once, but every day. Of course, these attachments include thoughts that are necessary to achieve your ideals, but you're required to reflect on them and see if they are truly necessary to your ideals or if they're actually just the source of your suffering.

This is what it means for an evil spirit to plug its cord into you. Without a doubt, that's the very thought that it will plug its cord into, and it's that thought that you will have to get rid of.

How to Abandon Your Attachments

What can you do to get rid of your attachments? As I had mentioned earlier on, one way of doing so is to change your thinking from seeking love from others to giving love to others. And if your feelings of inferiority run deep so that you're continually thinking about how unintelligent you are, another approach is to put a different thought in its place. Say to yourself, "If I have time to think about this, I'd be better off spending that time studying instead." You can also conquer your attachments by thinking, "All is transient in this world. This earthly world is this earthly world only, in the end, and I will be departing from it eventually. In the final analysis, only my soul's victory will remain." The victory of your soul will be the only thing remaining in the end. You may be defeated in this earthly world's terms, but that doesn't equal true defeat in life. Whatever other people may say about you, however society might judge you, and whatever your family may say to you in this earthly world, these are worldly judgments that have nothing to do with your defeat or triumph in life. In the final analysis, the final victory or defeat of your life is determined by the victory or defeat of your very soul. By looking at what determines success in life through the eyes of the world beyond this world, it's possible for you to abandon your attachments. And by doing so, you'll also admonish the evil spirits.

When an evil spirit possesses you, for example, other people appear in your eyes as bad people, and you'll say many words to speak ill of them. Words speaking ill of them come out of your mouth one after another. At that time, you have to think about whether these words are really your own or whether they could be those of the evil spirit. If you have a habit of speaking ill of others all the time, it's often an indication that an evil spirit from the Hell of Strife could be possessing you. In that case, the possessing spirit might not be just your own. You could be receiving the influence of one that's possessing another family member. It could, for example, be the spirit that's possessing your spouse or your parents if their vibrations are very harsh and they're constantly quarreling with each other. When someone like this lives around you, in some cases the spirit that's possessing them could jump to you. For this reason, you have to be very careful.

First, it's not a good sign if you have bouts of anger. It's also not a good sign if you're complaining a lot. You're likely possessed by an evil spirit if you're complaining, having constant feelings of frustration, or feeling angry all the time. The possession is the result of feelings of dissatisfaction with your environment or something else.

Therefore, as much as you can, shift your thinking from taking love from others to giving love to others. Rather than thinking of getting something from others or being recognized by people around you, change your mindset and think of what you, yourself, can do for other people. Then when there are things you cannot change through your own effort, it's important to feel indifferent to the situation. Think to yourself, "What belongs to this earthly world belongs to this earthly world, in the end," and don't let your heart become attached to transient matters. Keep a transparent heart like this, don't hold onto attachments, and live your life gracefully.

It's better to think in this way: "What has passed has passed, and I cannot change what's already gone by. But I can change the future. So, I'll work to change the changeable future. There are things about the past that I regret. I will self-reflect on those things, but I won't brood on things that I don't have the power to fix. It would be wrong of me to exaggerate them within my mind.

I will think of this life as just this life alone. And I will use the lessons I learn in this life in my next life and onward to make those lives better."

When the evil spirit detaches from you through your self-reflection, you will actually feel it peeling away from you. It really feels as though there is wallpaper being peeled off you. Even though spirits don't actually weigh anything, you physically feel heavy when an evil spirit is possessing you. Your physical body feels as if there is a heavy weight on you, and you'll feel a little unwell every day. You have a blue feeling, the way you feel on a rainy day during the monsoon season, when the sky is overcast and you're riding the crowded train. You feel physically groggy and can't get yourself to accomplish things. This is the way it feels when you're possessed by an evil spirit.

The moment this evil spirit peels away from you, the color will return to your face. When an evil spirit has created a spiritual disturbance inside you, your face will often look pale and ashen, like the signs of death. So, the moment you get rid of the evil spirit, a healthy flush will be restored to your face.

There will also be a light that flows into your body, and a wash of warmth will fill your body. Or as color returns to your face, you'll feel the warmth inside you, like the warmth of sunshine. Then you'll recognize that you feel much lighter than before. It's a heavy feeling, after all, to be carrying the suffering of one or sometimes even two or three evil spirits. It's because we human beings are spiritual beings. So, you'll feel much better when you're able to remove them.

But if you repeat your worries again and again, the evil spirit will come back to you, even if you were able to remove it once. For this reason, after the evil spirit goes away, it's very important to live with a bright outlook on your life as much as you're able to. It's important to do your best not to become in tune with the evil spirit's vibrations again. In conclusion, after you get rid of the evil spirit by practicing self-reflection, what you should do from then on is live a constructive and positive life to avoid tuning into the evil spirit's suffering vibrations again.

Being Prone to Spiritual Possession Is Unrelated to Intelligence

Whether you'll experience possession by evil spirits or not isn't related to your level of intelligence. It's not at all true to say that evil spirits can't possess intelligent people but can possess *un*intelligent people. Instead, it's basically related to the person's character. It's an issue of personal character. Evil spirits aren't able to easily possess good-natured people but can easily possess ill-natured people. I once read a book based on a conversation between anonymous government officials in a certain government ministry. Three officials were involved, and I could tell that all of them were under the possession of evil spirits from the Hell of Strife. I felt very unwell after reading that book and was unable to work on anything for half the day. They probably became possessed while being busy working. If they were to come into a room, I would probably sense a cloudy feeling entering the room, and it would feel as if something were sticking to me, and it would be a very difficult feeling to endure. As this story shows, whether you are intelligent or not isn't related to your proneness to spiritual possession.

When your mind is moving in huge waves and you've become very hostile toward others, you're absolutely apt to get possessed by an evil spirit from the Hell of Strife. Then, you might be led to take your own life, or, if the possession is even stronger, you might harass others. You'll behave in one of these two ways.

Whether you receive spiritual influence from evil spirits or your guardian spirit isn't related to your intelligence in the worldly sense of the word. It's mainly an issue of your personal character. To put it another way, it's related to how steady your emotions are or, said another way, how steady your life perspective is. This is what's related to spiritual possession.

Therefore, it's untrue to say that you'll become possessed by an evil spirit if you're unintelligent and you'll receive inspirations from high heavenly spirits if you're smart. This is not the case at all. This is entirely an issue about your character as a person.

It's also good to keep in mind that worries are also unrelated to your intelligence. Worries are things you experience whether you are intelligent or unintelligent. This is especially true of the emotional kinds of worries. For example, problems in relationships with the opposite sex aren't related to your IQ score. Whether your

IQ is 100 or 200, you'll experience problems in relationships with the opposite sex, either way.

We human beings are prone to spiritual disturbances related to emotional problems, so we need to be careful about these problems. There are characteristics that we each are born with, in this regard. But what is essential is to look at yourself carefully and objectively and work to keep your emotions under control.

I have talked about the principle of self-reflection. This principle is also teaching that you, yourself, are the main actor who can break through your spiritual disturbance as you strive to enter the path to happiness, the path to enlightenment. It all begins with yourself, in the end.

5

The Principle of Progress—
Your Thoughts Become Reality

Your Good Thoughts but Also
Your Bad Thoughts Become Reality

Fourth, I would like to talk about your thoughts becoming reality. This is a teaching related to the principle of progress, and there are variations to this principle depending on each person's stage of life. It's difficult to discuss, because the best way to apply this principle to your life depends on where you're currently standing in life.

But basically, I can say that we, human beings, are spiritual beings after all, and the world of spirits is a world of thought. It's a place where thoughts become reality. Those in the other world who have hellish thoughts are living in and creating hell together with many other beings. By creating a sadistic and masochistic world, the beings living in hell make each other suffer. On the other hand, the beings living in heaven are supporting each other in their world.

In this way, the other world is a place where thoughts become reality, and in truth, the other world is the actual world. Thoughts are the actual nature of human beings. And our physical bodies are vessels and a means to carry us so we can make our thoughts a reality. It's necessary to think of who we are in this way.

Because this world is a material world, your thoughts require some time to actualize in this earthly world. In this world, cars are essential transportation to get from one place to another. It's the same with trying to make your thoughts a reality—we have to use various material means and objects to make things happen. For example, if you were in the spirit world, you would be able to get from Tokyo to Nagoya City immediately, the very instant you thought about it. Indeed, it takes only one moment to get there. There is a proverb that says, "One thought leads to three thousand worlds," and it's true, whether you want to go to heaven or to hell. It's indeed true that you will go anywhere the second that you think about it. It's almost scary how barrierless time and space are in the spirit world.

In my case, when I look at a photo of someone who's not living anymore, I get attuned to them within a second. This person could be living in heaven or hell, it doesn't matter where. It takes just a second for me to connect with them. So, it's better if I stay interested in spirits living in the higher worlds of heaven as much as I can. When a spirit comes to me from higher heaven, I can also give a spiritual message from that spirit. But if I think too much about and connect with a spirit residing in hell, the spirit might not leave me easily, which is extremely uncomfortable for me. When that happens, it's important to me to avoid holding any interest in the spirit.

Such a world unmistakably exists. The people of this earthly world are making their thoughts a reality too, in the end. According to the same principle that gives rise to heaven and hell in the other world, our thoughts become reality no matter whether they're the good or the bad kind. There could be heavenly thoughts and hellish thoughts, and whatever quality of thought they are, they become actualized. For example, if someone has the wish to kill someone, they might eventually do so. But even if they don't put their thought into action, they might encounter this kind of crime and end up becoming the one who's killed instead. In this way, holding bad thoughts inside you will always attract bad results.

If everyone had thoughts about making other people happy and lived their lives in this way, a heaven would, indeed, be created. It's a fact. A heaven will appear here if the number of such people increases. But if everyone wished for people to be *un*happy and wanted to make people *un*happy, it would create a hell. That's the nature of the world we live in. Thoughts will become a reality whether those thoughts are of good quality or bad quality. This is the truth of the spirit world, after all.

Regarding this world, there are material hindrances to this happening, which slows the process down a little bit. It doesn't necessarily happen straightaway, partly because there are other people involved. But people's thoughts always become reality in the long term, after 10, 20, or 30 years have passed. Like flowing lava, your thoughts gradually solidify. And there may be some variations in its color and degree, but after all is said and done, people will manifest things into this world according to the direction of their thoughts. Good things get manifested, and bad things get manifested as well.

Every day, progress is made in the direction of everyone's own curiosities and interests. This also is an unmistakable truth and the reality of human life. It's an essential thing to know concerning the principle of progress. It's essential to know that there is a principle of thoughts existing in this world, and our good thoughts and bad thoughts become realities. To put it another way, having bad thoughts attracts bad results, and having good thoughts attracts good results. This, indeed, is the result you will always see, based on the principles of the spirit world. This is why it's essential to learn what's good and what's wrong and to realize that your thoughts have the power to become a reality.

Love, Wisdom, and Self-Reflection
Are Ways to Progress

If you have looked inside your mind deeply and envisioned the love, wisdom, and self-reflection I mentioned earlier on, the result will appear through this principle of progress. As a result of deeply correcting yourself through the principle of love, the principle of wisdom, and the principle of self-reflection, you will move forward according to the principle of progress.

If your thoughts are all about taking love from others and you work very hard to manifest those thoughts, your life will tend in the direction that makes yourself and other people *un*happy. This is the principle of love. The principle of wisdom, too, dictates that if your thoughts are heading in the wrong direction, the result will be unhappiness. If you understand self-reflection, then your thoughts will head in a righteous direction, but if you don't practice self-reflection, your thoughts will head in the wrong direction. In this way, when you have cleared each of the principles, which are love, wisdom, and self-reflection, and have done so in the right way, you will then move on to the principle of progress and will move forward in the right direction. You will make your progress in the direction of loving others. The various things you learn through the principle of wisdom will contribute to your progress, too. And you will enter the path of progress through self-reflection if you have been thinking to yourself, "I will look at the mistakes of my life, or the mistakes I've made and the worries I am having, and solve them one by one. I'll look at these problems and study and examine them to find the answers to them."

The principles of love, wisdom, and self-reflection are all ways of entering the path of progress. If you go down these paths before you enter the path of progress, you'll avoid making huge mistakes.

Seek the Kind of Happiness that Also Leads to Others' Happiness

First, you must believe that thoughts will always become realities. Over the course of 10, 20, or 30 years, your thoughts will always become manifested. Even if your thoughts fail to come to completion in this world, they will still manifest themselves later in the spirit world.

For example, in an earthly sense, Jesus Christ strove to become a savior but died on the cross instead. If you look at this event only through the eyes of this world, it may seem that his thoughts didn't become reality. It may seem he failed to fulfill his missionary work. His twelve disciples also betrayed him and escaped in the end. It's famous that Judas sold out Jesus for monetary gain, but even the other disciples feared persecution and escaped, pretending they didn't know Jesus. In this sense, when we see how his physical life met its end in this earthly world, it seems as if Jesus's thoughts ended in defeat, that his mission was a kind of failure. But over a long course of time, his wish as a savior came true. It's essential to know that thoughts sometimes won't succeed in becoming realities if we focus only on a certain span of time. But they will almost certainly become a reality over the course of a long period.

In Jesus's case, he had realized that kind of wish as a savior, but I also recognize the impact of the tragic aspect inside him that influenced these 2,000 years of human history. There are righteous religions, but each is marked by its own qualities, and in Jesus's case, there was an extremely tragic and end-of-times quality within him. I think that since his time, there have been a lot of elements along that line that have manifested.

It's very important in Happy Science how we send thoughts out from ourselves and where we direct them. It's essential to always be thinking about what kinds of thoughts we're having, what kinds of realities our thoughts will bring forth, and what will unfold as a result of our thoughts. It's especially important to consider what will result from acting on certain thoughts if they created a huge influential trend. Our final goal, after all, is to gather our thoughts in the direction of the happiness of all people. In Happy Science, we say, "We are seeking the happiness of all humankind. We are seeking our happiness in order to make all people's happiness a reality." So, we must have thoughts that say, "When I achieve happiness, it will be the kind that leads to the happiness of all people everywhere.

I seek a way of life in which the accomplishment of my own happiness leads to the happiness of people all around the world." If these are your thoughts, then you won't make a mistake when these thoughts become reality. It's important to live with thoughts that say, "I pray for my path to happiness to unite with the happiness of all humankind."

The number of people who are not seeking this way of self-realization and who are actualizing wrong things are endless. Even if they seem to attain success in the earthly sense, if they're not practicing the right mind, they could be manifesting wrong things into reality. If money is all you wish for, then you might decide to commit a bank robbery or fraud.

If you aspire to make your happiness coincide with the happiness of all people over 10 or 20 years of effort, a trend in that direction will gradually emerge, and that trend will ultimately lead to the actualization of your aspiration. During this time, always check, "Will this happiness I seek lead to the happiness of all people? Are my thoughts free of wrongs? Are they headed in a righteous direction?" If you can say yes to these questions, your thoughts will always become actualized over a long course of time.

The degree to which your thoughts are manifested into reality will depend on your earnestness and effort in combination with adequate time. It will be determined by the earnestness of your thoughts. It will be determined by how much effort you will make based on your earnestness. And it will be determined by the time you spend continuing your efforts. Earnestness, effort, and time—through the sum of these things, your thoughts will definitely be realized.

This is what I can say regarding the principle of progress.

6

The Four Principles to Happiness Are Spiritual Training for Your Life

Everything I have discussed in this chapter is based on my real-life experiences, and I'm certain that all of you will also experience these four principles in actuality. Besides what I have discussed in this chapter, the principles of happiness contain numerous deep teachings, which have been taught in various other books I've published. In this particular chapter, I've explained this principle under the theme of "The Four Principles of Human Happiness" and approached it by discussing topics that are simple to understand.

You could use this chapter's advice in your missionary work, or you could use it in your own self-reflection and meditation; for example, you could use particular phrases as contemplation themes. You could spend time in a seminar meditating on "freeing yourself from the suffering of taking love from others" as a topic for your contemplation. You could also contemplate the themes, "If you have time to wish you were more intelligent, use that time to study," "Self-reflection can cut off evil spiritual disturbances," and, "Thoughts become reality." As you do so, you will see your spiritual training in life progress even further.

CHAPTER FOUR

INTRODUCTION TO HAPPY SCIENCE

The Mindsets to Happiness for All People

1

How Happy Science Began

We Started with Limited Membership, Then We Shifted to Letting Many Join

More than 10 years have now passed since the beginning of Happy Science's activities.* The number of books I've published during this period is in the hundreds, and the number of my lectures totals more than several hundred.† With this enormous body of Truths, people who newly enter Happy Science might feel as if they're swimming in a great sea of Truths and may feel lost about where they should begin studying. I've written this chapter, entitled "Introduction to Happy Science," at this time of more than 10 years after the founding of Happy Science, so that I myself can talk about the meaning of becoming a member and our basic teachings.

My teachings are very vast, if I say so myself, so this might become a discussion of the basics of the basics, in the end. But I think that it will, at the very least, help you get a general understanding of our basic thinking. In Happy Science, I have developed various

---

* TF: At the time this book's Japanese edition was published on January 7, 2004.

† TF: The number of books and lectures mentioned here was accurate at the time this book's Japanese edition was published on January 7, 2004. As of July 2020, Master Okawa has given more than 3,150 lectures and published more than 2,700 titles.

kinds of teachings, but it was not done without rhyme or reason. When I look back at my early lectures, I see that the idea of the principles of happiness has appeared since my very first public lecture. Since then, I have also spoken in turn about the other principles, such as the principle of love, and the others which we call the ten principles.*

At the start of things, I set up an examination system to limit membership to Happy Science. I set up an application system so that not everyone wishing to join could do so. I did this to ensure we admitted people who were suited to studying my teachings and were not intending to create disturbances, were serious about joining, or weren't coming to disrupt other members' journeys. So, I asked those who wanted to join us to read my books of the Truths and write about their aspirations for going through soul training at Happy Science. I asked them to write about their purpose for joining and to compose an essay about our most basic books. And in the beginning, I evaluated these essays myself.

In the beginning, if there were 100 people wanting to join and submitting essays to me, the admittance rate came to about 40 percent. Forty percent of people were allowed to pass and join, and another 50 percent were put on the waiting list. Those on the waiting list were asked to spend another six months further studying my teachings, reading my books, and practicing a little self-reflection, and were asked to apply again after that. This was the waiting list system we had set up. And finally, there was about 10

---

* TF: See Ryuho Okawa, *The Science of Happiness* (Vermont: Destiny Books, 2009).

percent of applicants who I could tell from their applications were under spiritual disturbance or were somewhat mentally disturbed from going to too many other religious organizations. These types of people were also drawn to us from reading my spiritual messages, and I felt that letting them enter Happy Science too easily could disrupt the other members. That was the reason I gave a notice of unacceptance to about 10 percent of applicants.

In the beginning, a large number of the people who were put on the waiting list went on to become executives of Happy Science, and I felt sorry that they had initially been waitlisted. But afterward, they told me that they had learned a lot from that experience, because it helped them avoid becoming overly arrogant. Those who became Happy Science staff or members ahead of them appeared admirable, and they envied them.

In this way, my aim in the beginning was not to enlarge the organization too much. Instead, I first wanted to develop a good organization. The image I had at first was to gather a membership numbering in the several thousands, develop this membership into a solid and good organization, and then steadily grow its size to 10,000 members. Then, once our reputation reached a certain level and the organization's methods of operation became solidly established, I would expand the organization further. So, the first three years of Happy Science's development were carefully controlled. Of course, it took time to learn how to operate the organization, and even though I went to these lengths to contain its growth, we saw explosive energy entering our organization and pushing us forward, which gave us quite a difficult time with our management operations.

On a personal level, I, myself, wished to write more about my basic teachings, and I knew that this would be difficult if I were to become too busy to put my thoughts together. So, I set forth my basic ways of thinking and asked just the people who resonated with them to join and work with us. I thought that admitting someone who'd only read one spiritual message might have some risks. They might not be so reliable, even if they became a member. This is why I asked those who wanted to join to study a certain number of my books first—so we could be certain that they hadn't misunderstood my teachings.

Sure enough, in the beginning, there were a handful of people with religious leanings who didn't have the right understanding, and this led them to stumble. They were able to accept most of my teachings, but they refused to accept certain parts of them, so they weren't able to enter Happy Science. Seeing this, I was glad that I had practiced caution in the beginning.

But, in the end, the mission of a religion is, after all, to spread the teachings. While there's always some risk in accepting people who have issues, I felt that we would be able to handle them as the organization grew in size. In this way, we eventually entered the stage of salvation during the 1990s with the mission to save all humankind and spread our activities. When we began our activities in other countries, we were told that a religion requiring an evaluation to enter the membership was unheard of. Some

THE LAWS *of* HAPPINESS

people said that it wouldn't be a religion if it required that because a religion's work is to increase its number of believers as much as possible, and that that is how religions serve the public good. To people abroad, we appeared more like a school. It is true that, at first, we began with a school-like system.

To put it another way, there were voices from overseas asking for more admissions and approval to let many more people join, and I could understand their feeling. They said, "It isn't like a religion to refuse to allow so many people to join. Please let more people join. Other bad places are brainwashing people to join them. It doesn't make sense for a good religion to be so hesitant to include more people. I won't recognize you as a religion unless you allow more and more people to join Happy Science." So I said, "Okay, then, I'll allow more people to join."

In other words, we weren't prepared to accept more members, in actuality. But this also means that we were gathering a lot of popularity as a religion from the very start. I think that we were a very popular religion.

The Number of My Believers Grew through My Books

My books have often ranked number one in actual sales on a yearly basis. But the distributors have strived hard to prevent my books from becoming the number one bestseller, and they seem to always be working hard to rank several other books above mine. They have to do so, since it's true that we may become a target of jealousy if my books always rank number one.

The jealousy that arises from major publishing companies and other authors is quite severe, so the distributors have to put forth a lot of effort to help these publishers save face. So, they rank several of the major publishers at the very top and place my books third or fourth when other publishers are peaceful, but they downgrade my books to tenth place when other publishers begin complaining. According to a professional, they may have been manipulating the rankings in this way, but in truth, my books have actually always ranked number one over the past several years. My books have been the number one bestsellers in Japan. In some sense, this is an unfair situation, and it shows that freedom of religion is not rooted yet in Japan. It's considered against ethical values to let religions spread.

In the United States, books published by new thought religious leaders such as Norman Vincent Peale and Robert Schuller have ranked openly as the number one best-selling books, including in the newspaper rankings. In the United States it's actually common to find books by religious leaders ranking number one. It's considered only natural for religious books to become bestsellers, so they are probably not being discriminated against in the United States.

The reason such publications are treated negatively in Japan is probably that people believe that religious organizations are forcing their believers to purchase their books. But in the case of

Happy Science, we began by limiting our members first, and when my books became best-selling books, this led to the growth of our membership. This has become the basis of our confidence.

My books were constantly selling and creating a hidden, outside "membership" about 10 times the size of our actual membership. It was not that I had an existing organization of believers created by a predecessor to help my books become bestsellers. When I held public lectures in the beginning, only about 10 to 30 percent of my audiences were from our actual membership. The rest of the people in the audience weren't members, and I was still able to gather audiences of tens of thousands of people. For this reason, we had a lot of confidence.

Other religious organizations are just asking their members to purchase their books in bulk even if those books aren't selling well, and the distributors wouldn't rank these books at the top. But, in my case, we began with my books from the outset, in the first place. And then the growth of my following came afterward. As the number of my believers grew more than I expected it would, we had no choice but to prepare our organization to accept them. This was the process that our religious organization went through.

This is the reason why I think that our case is different from others. If I become too involved in managing the organization, it will be harder to hold lectures. I feel that we should enlarge our membership at cruising speed to some degree.

Now we have entered the stage of salvation and our style of operation has changed, but our original spirit remains the same.

As much as possible, I would like for myself to remember the importance of the height of my teachings and the diligence of our members' efforts in studying them. I would like us to have this as our starting point, after all. And I want people who make efforts and discipline themselves to guide other people.

2

Exploration of the Right Mind and the Principles of Happiness

The Laws of the Mind that Make People Happy or Unhappy

I've held numerous lectures, more than I could actually count. Even so, I have never given the same lecture more than once. That is my style. All my lectures are different from one another. This might make it difficult for members to learn them all. But this decision comes from my inner conscience. It feels important for me to have the mindset of putting my heart into each new lecture as if I'm creating a new masterpiece.

I am accumulating one teaching after another on themes that are essential to people's enlightenment and happiness. I'm completing them one by one, as I notice one topic and then another that could be important to people.

Just as I had foreseen, the teachings that resonate with members are different for each person. People are moved by various books. One person is moved by one book, but another person is moved by another book. Even in the same book, there are different parts that people react to. Their hearts are saved by different parts of the book. This is how things have been.

Even if I might feel that something might not be necessary to say, I still decide to say it in case it could ever lead to saving someone. And when I do, people have appeared who were saved by those words precisely. For the most part, each time I think to myself, "Maybe this isn't necessary to say," there are several tens to several hundreds of people who feel saved by those words, after all.

When I give lectures, many people believe I am talking about them, that I could be referring to them personally, and that I could be pointing out their mistakes or scolding them. Many people feel this way. But I don't actually know them by face, and I'm not necessarily personally admonishing them.

This is just the way the Laws are. They strike many people's hearts. They strike their mistakes. They encourage people. They call on them to rebuild their lives. This is what is contained within my Laws.

By always watching how people's minds waver, I'm continually seeking for the laws which have universal aspects. I have been teaching in many different ways the constant laws of the mind within the diversity of human life in this world, and have been teaching that through living by these laws, we human beings will become happier. And when we sway off the course of these laws, we will become *un*happier. I have been teaching these laws in various ways with the wish that you will encounter this chance, that at some point you will be touched by the chance for enlightenment. The contents of my teachings have addressed diverse subjects, but even as diverse as they have been, the singular laws of the mind persist through all of them.

My mind has always been thinking about the laws of the mind. There are laws for becoming happier. There are also laws for becoming unhappier. So, what are these laws? Sometimes, I have discussed these laws by describing individual, specific examples to help you understand them inductively. Sometimes I have tried to help you understand them deductively, for example by saying, "God's heart is such and such, and so you can become happier through living in this way." I have used both approaches, but the laws of the mind have always been central.

The True Meaning of Righteousness

From the beginning, I have called this approach to the mind that makes people happier "Exploration of the Right Mind." It's difficult to say it simply, but this righteousness we seek, in the end, is a mind that accords with the Laws of the Original God who created the great universe. And this righteousness, of course, includes the heart of belief, which can only be approached through religion. In this sense, the rightness I am referring to does not necessarily coincide with the rightness of this material world.

The righteousness of this material world includes the theories, hypotheses, and academic propositions of the scientific world. We're told about scientific findings, but, to me, even these things are just one academic theory or one hypothesis. They are just one opinion that has not been fully proven to be true.

I, myself, don't believe what scientific experts say, whether they tell me that human beings were born tens of thousands of years ago or that human beings and chimpanzees evolutionarily diverged four million years ago. I don't believe either of these to be the real truth.

As long as this is what is being taught in school, you can't help but mark this on your exams as the correct answer. Schools will need to mark them as the correct answers. But school textbooks are not always correct. Since the education ministry (in Japan) approves them at this time, I don't intend to say anything about them. But the righteousness we seek doesn't always coincide with these kinds of scientific or academic results and studies.

I don't want to say this too strongly, because I don't want it to lead to trouble in the schools. I believe that what's taught at school can be followed at school, and matters that fall outside school education can be pursued outside of school education. There are rules in this world, so just as Jesus said while looking at a coin, "Render to Caesar the things that are Caesar's and to God the things that are God's," I don't want to fuss too much about what's running smoothly in this world.*

But righteousness, in the true meaning of the word, is based on a belief in God's existence and an understanding of the spirit world. In this sense, righteousness cannot be found in school textbooks.

Even what we have been calling science has not yet successfully proved the existence of spirits. More than 2,500 years ago, Shakyamuni Buddha—in search of answers to questions about birth, aging, illness, and death—left his home. But even now, modern medicine has not found the real meaning of being born into this world. Now, 2,500 years later, modern medicine has not discovered what death means and cannot tell us about the world after death. We cannot deny that there is still a great need for religion. In this sense, I do not feel that what is being said in science, medicine, and education is perfectly righteous. But I don't want to debate about them to the point that they'll stop existing or providing a livelihood to those who work in those fields.

But it's important to have a sense of righteousness that's based on the world of religious faith. While we are living in this earthly world, there are certain ways to get through this life. For example, there are doctors who have religious faith, but when performing surgery, they will need to use a materialistic approach. They're required to practice the use of medicine and the surgical removal

---

* TF: This was the author's stance in 2004. Now, Happy Science conducts various activities in the educational area.

of ailing parts. It's what's being practiced in the medical world, so this materialistic approach is permitted as a means to get through this world. But I will say straightforwardly that it doesn't offer enough understanding of the soul, of the fundamental nature of human beings.

The same thing is true of society's laws and constitutional law. Constitutions weren't written by God. They were created by human beings, after all, and determined by the legislative body of countries according to majority rule. Depending on the congressional landscape, conclusions will vary. Conclusions change depending on which party holds the majority of congressional seats. In this sense, these decisions are not necessarily absolutely right. There are judges and lawyers. But I recognize that their righteousness differs from the righteousness of the religious world.

At the same time, I've also said, when I was publishing the spiritual message series, that the righteousness I was referring to is not the kind that says, "Only this can be righteous." The different high spirits have differences in personalities and perspectives. The *Ryuho Okawa Great Collections* of spiritual messages have proved that.

The high spirits have surpassed a certain spiritual level. And they have a way of thinking that makes people happier. So, in this regard, they have fulfilled a condition of heaven. But they have differences in their methods and thinking. And which way of thinking will make people happier will be different depending on each individual person.

So, if you look at the religion's influential power, you can recognize which one has more righteousness overall or which one you can believe in. But since there are various ways of thinking showing that people have that much variety in their needs, I am not here to deny that fact.

I recognize that there is a plurality to what is right. But at the same time, there is a one and only heart of God that we are working toward within this plurality of righteousness. This is the kind of righteousness that I teach.

The Principles of Happiness: The Modern Fourfold Path

I've taught the principles of happiness as concrete teachings for exploring the right mind.

You may want to ask me then, "What does it mean to seek for a righteous mind?" I would answer by saying, "It's to seek the principles of happiness." And if you focus on the principles of happiness and make efforts, you will become happy.

The principles of happiness is a principle that is not on its own but is a way of thinking containing other principles. The first is the principle of love. The second is the principle of wisdom, the third is the principle of self-reflection, and the fourth is the principle of progress. Aside from these, I've spoken about many additional principles, so there are, of course, many ways to become happier, an overflowing number of ways. But if I were to sum up the principles of happiness, they would come down to love, wisdom, self-reflection, and progress. I call these four principles "The Modern Fourfold Path."

Please follow these four principles. If you follow these four principles, always remembering to seek for a righteous mind, you will avoid wandering too far off the righteous course and you'll at least be able to enter heaven. From there, you will be able to train to become an angel of light. This was the reason behind my giving the teaching the "principles of happiness."

If you are a member of Happy Science, I ask you to explore the right mind, which is another way of saying to seek your divine nature. And I ask that you seek the principles of happiness—love, wisdom, self-reflection, and progress—as your specific goal, as your day-to-day practice.

Therefore, if I were asked what the basic teachings of Happy Science are, I would answer, "Happy Science asks all believers to seek for a righteous mind. And on a concrete level, as a way to practice this mind, we teach them to practice the principles of happiness. There are four principles of happiness: love, wisdom, self-reflection, and progress. You will get accepted as a Happy Science believer if you can follow these principles. Please don't forget this teaching, and always keep this teaching in mind as you study the

Truths; in your self-reflection, prayer, and missionary work; and as a member of society. For if you do, you will not wander far from the righteous path, and you will be making daily efforts as a believer." This is the kind of structure I gave my teachings.

3

The Principle of Love

Love that Gives, Not Love that Takes

The first principle is the principle of love. The principles of happiness could be constructed in different ways. But since it's the first of the principles, I wanted it to be a broad gateway, a teaching that would be wide enough to allow anyone to practice. Those who are studious and intelligent may wish for more complex discussions about how to reach enlightenment. But not all people are well-learned, and in reality, people who are suffering aren't necessarily suffering rationally—they're suffering emotionally. So, I felt that the principle that's the largest, most universal one throughout the world is the principle of love. It is the broadest one and one that people can easily start with. But it is by no means an inferior principle. It's a gateway to my teachings that anyone can start with but no one can graduate from. This is the principle of love.

The principle of love contains many teachings to be given. But first and foremost, I have taught these words to help you attain enlightenment: "Do you think that love is something to be taken from others? Do you see love as something that you gain from other people, as something to get from someone else?" That's not truly love.

You're suffering because you are thinking about getting something from others. This is the "love" that early Buddhism of long ago called attachment. It's the "love" that's in the shape of an attachment. And the love that I have been teaching, the "love that gives," was called not by the word *love*, but by the word *compassion* in early Buddhism. The love that I am teaching, therefore, is not the love of an attachment, but the love of compassion.

Compassion only knows to give. It never seeks return; it only keeps giving. I have been calling it "love that gives" as a way to easily understand it in a worldly sense. I could have chosen to call it by the word compassion, but that's an older word that people may not easily understand nowadays. So, to translate it into modern terms, I call it "love that gives." This is a phrase that elementary school and middle school students can also understand.

It is saying, "When you hear the word *love*, almost all of you think of being loved by the man you admire, by the woman you admire, by your parents, by your children. It's all thoughts about getting love from others. But because you cannot get enough love from them, you suffer. You need to solve this."

If everyone were to think only about getting love from others and there were no one to provide the love, of course, there wouldn't be enough love for everyone in this world. This is why we need to begin by supplying love. If each person could supply others with love, love would overfill this world. So, we must stop thinking about always getting love from others.

Many people are like ill patients lying in the hospital, receiving treatment, and saying how much pain they are in and how much they need more medicine. It's this state that many people find themselves facing in a society without enough love. This is what everyone is saying in a society of love that takes. Of course, this poses problems. More doctors and nurses become necessary. More medicine also becomes necessary.

So, instead of that, let's give love to others from wherever we can begin. Let's work for the benefit of other people. Before saying how much we want to be happy, let's make efforts to make other people happy.

When the number of people who do these things grows, your problems will automatically be solved. Most suffering comes from your attachments. You wish for others to do certain things, but they don't. This kind of suffering is called "the pain of unfulfillment" in Buddhism. Among Shakyamuni Buddha's teachings, this is his teaching on suffering, and it says that in this world there are things that we cannot have, however much we want to have them. If we continually seek to have these things, we will find no one in this world who is happy. So, let's begin from somewhere we can begin. Begin with practicing the love that gives to others. By doing so, a path will open up to you.

People practicing love that gives have taken a step forward on the path of happiness already. First, each day will feel happy for you. Next, seeing others becoming happy will make you also feel happier. If you can feel happier from seeing other people become happier, this means that you have also taken one step forward on the road to heaven. It's people with this heart who will go to heaven.

Those who become envious or jealous when they see other people becoming happier are in the wrong. The heart of wishing happiness only for yourself, the heart that doesn't want others to find happiness and that wishes *un*happiness on others instead, is the heart of hell. This is why people with a heart that feels joy in seeing other people becoming happier have fulfilled the condition for entering heaven. This means that by mastering even just the first principle, the principle of love, the gates of heaven will open to you. This will be enough to open them. Therefore, it seems simple. But it's deep and tremendously profound.

There Are Developmental Stages to Love

To take this teaching on love further, I have also discussed the different stages of love in *The Laws of the Sun*[*]. It begins with fundamental love, then nurturing love, followed by forgiving love,

---

[*] TF: See Ryuho Okawa, *The Laws of the Sun* (New York: IRH Press, 2018).

and finally love incarnate. This may sound difficult. It may seem like a complicated philosophical discussion, but it's not necessarily.

The first one is fundamental love. It's a love for your neighbors, family, friends, and those who are around you every day. It may seem to be an inferior type of love, but this is not actually the case. All who practice this love will gain entrance into heaven, so this is a tremendously large gateway of the Truths. It's essential to begin by practicing fundamental love.

Next, there is nurturing love. This is a love one stage above the state of mind that has already entered heaven. There is a stern aspect to this love, and it requires the use of wisdom. This love is the love of a leader, the love that comes from those who guide others. For example, the love of a schoolteacher isn't a love that is always easygoing with the children. Receiving praise and being treated kindly, of course, makes children feel happy, but this is not enough when you are on the side of educating people. Children need to be reprimanded when a reprimand is necessary. Children need to change aspects of themselves that need to be changed. It might be very difficult for them to experience this, but as a teacher, it is important to teach them that if they don't make efforts now, their paths may not open up to them.

This love that combines kindness with sternness through wisdom is nurturing love. If you are able to reach this stage of love, you will become a splendid leader in the earthly sense.

In addition to that, there is the religious state of love, which is called forgiving love. This is a far deeper love that comes. Up to nurturing love is the farthest you can reach when thinking about yourself, your sense of self, the self as being separate and independent of others.

But when you reach a higher state, the religious state of love, you will feel that you are yourself, but also not yourself. You will feel as if you're living upon the palms of God's great hands and you are being given your life. You will also feel that you are living in this earthly world as one of His fingers, that you are here to carry out your life in this world as each one of the fingers on His hands. This is the feeling you will begin to understand. It is the feeling that you are not yourself.

You will feel that you were chosen by God to fulfill part of His mission. This deeply profound view of your life in this world will grow inside you. And when this profound view of life grows, your view of the world will fill with the heart of mercy. Your heart will be moved, as you notice how all the living beings of this world are going through their own soul training.

You will be able to see the light of goodness and the light of divine nature within people, no matter how wrongful they may be. You will be able to see that there is divine nature also inside such people, but some kind of a wrongful thinking and wrongful heart has led them to commit wrongful deeds, and they are suffering as a result. You will wonder to yourself if there could be some way that they could make their divine nature shine. And you will think to yourself that no matter how much they are unloved by others, you will love the light of divine nature within them. So, when this heart grows within you, you will feel the heart of love and the heart of compassion toward wrongful people.

In addition, you will feel moved by seeing all the living beings such as the flowers in the fields and the animals that are living in this world with all their might. You will also feel God's light within them. You'll realize that animals are also undergoing spiritual training in this world and striving throughout their lives. They are thinking of clever ways to obtain food, putting their all into protecting themselves from enemies, and doing all they can to raise their children. On the snowy days of winter, they go out in search of scarce grass for food, almost freezing to death. They live through their hardships as best they can. They do all they can to survive throughout their lives. They persevere through such kinds of difficulties as they strive to make their souls progress another level.

Their journey to becoming human is long, but within them there exists fundamentally the same essence. Inside, they have the same feelings of delight, anger, sorrow, and pleasure as human beings. You will look on these animals and recognize that they are wishing to someday become human beings over a very long course of reincarnations. You will come to recognize the life of God within all living beings. This stage of enlightenment is the world of forgiving love within you. When you reach this stage, you will be able to recognize things that you weren't able to see clearly during the stages up to nurturing love, and feelings of forgiving love will begin arising within you.

Then, above forgiving love, there is love incarnate, the stage of a tathagata's love. This is a tremendously vast state of mind, and it's not something you have to think about yet. Please put as much effort as possible into practicing fundamental love, nurturing love, and forgiving love.

Someone who has the state of love incarnate is someone whose very existence in this world becomes the spirit of the times they live in and shines light upon the world. It may not be a state of love that we can seek of our own will. It's something that the people of the world or that later generations will determine about someone. It's not something we ought to seek after. But we can pray to become an embodiment of love, to become like the sun above us, which shines light upon all of life in this world. We can seek to become an embodiment of mercy, like a raincloud pouring blessed rain upon the dry, drought-stricken land, showering vast lands with nourishing rain. This is the wish to become love incarnate. It's the wish to shine light upon as many people as possible, not only the people who are living near or around you.

We hold many activities at Happy Science, but our earthly work has faced limits. We have been publishing bestsellers, but there are people that these books haven't reached yet. There are people we still cannot reach, even if we hold public lectures. There are people we cannot reach even if we produce CDs. There are people we still cannot reach even if we publish foreign-language translations. There are a great many people in this world. But inside me I have the wish to convey the Truths to as many people as possible and help them become happier. It's my wish to accomplish this very vast task, and I believe that you wish to do this, too.

From the viewpoint of having the vast heart of mercy or feelings of great compassion, getting along with your family members and friends may seem to be a small form of love, it's true. This stage of love of loving the people near you may seem very small. But it's essential to take this first step in the beginning and let your heart of compassion grow vast over time. In this way, love has developmental stages.

Of course, there are common elements running through all stages of love. Fundamental love includes some aspects of nurturing love. Within nurturing love, there is fundamental love and also forgiving love. I'm sure that everyone has also become a small version of love incarnate. So, it's essential that you first become love incarnate within your home. You need to shine with light as a father or as a mother. You need to shine with light as children, and also shine light upon others at school or in your neighborhood. In this sense, everyone can be a small version of love incarnate. So, even though each stage of love is different from the other kinds of love, they are also the same.

It's a way of seeing: there are different levels of love that can be manifested, and there are some aspects of all levels inside each of us. It's just a matter of which level is manifesting most strongly in you.

Therefore, in my teaching on the developmental stages of love, I combined the stages of love with the stages of enlightenment. The principle of love teaches us to first abandon taking love from others and, instead, to devote our lives to loving others.

When the Principle of Love Spreads, There Will Be Peace on Earth

I assure you that if you practice this one principle throughout your life, you will be admitted into heaven. It's a teaching to be thankful for.

But if you lack wisdom in practicing this principle you will sometimes make mistakes. Sometimes, if you are too easygoing with others, it could encourage their downfall. Or if you give others praise for wrongful behavior, it could lead to aggrandizing their bad behavior. If such cases arise, you will need to use wisdom to sometimes admonish them, however reluctant you may be to do so. There will be times when you will have to reprimand them, guide them, and show them a sterner side of yourself. It's sometimes essential to show them the "stern father" side of yourself. This is nurturing love, which you will also need to learn to practice.

Then, if your practice of nurturing love becomes strong, your effort to distinguish good from evil becomes emphasized. When you are too particular about labeling people as good or evil, your heart can stray far from the true mind of God. It's your heart of forgiving love that will surpass this, in the end. The heart of deep compassion toward all living beings in this world will let you surpass the heart of nurturing love.

In addition to that, please desire to leave behind the vastest light possible during your handful of decades or the 100 years of your life in this world. Please desire to give your light to as many people as possible. Please desire to be a candle to light up the darkness as much as you can with the light of the Truths. Please desire to be a lighthouse on the harbor that shines its light as far into the distance as possible.

As a seeker of the Truths, it's essential to always keep the Developmental Stages of Love in your mind. In real life, however, you will probably stumble, even from the outset. Even if you want to practice love incarnate, you may experience conflicts with your spouse, parents, brothers, sisters, friends, or superiors. You may experience jealousy among your colleagues. Many things can happen to prevent things from working out as you wish they would.

This means that even when you feel you've finished one stage of love, this is not the end of your discipline. Your starting point is always the same, regardless. And the same things will arise again and again as opportunities for you to examine yourself and continue your spiritual training.

I have explained the principle of love. If people practice this one principle, there will be peace in the world. And it will also provide the world with a teaching that can't be found in the Christian teachings of love. Christianity teaches love, but because something is missing in it, it has led to endless conflicts. When the teachings of Buddhist love are added and the Christian teachings change to teachings of compassion, you will see conflicts subside. When this teaching of love spreads throughout the world, humanity will find more happiness.

4

The Principle of Wisdom

Turn Your Knowledge
into Wisdom through Experiences

The second principle of the principles of happiness is the principle of wisdom. In these modern times, we are living in a great information society. And throughout your soul's journey of reincarnations, I don't think there will be any better time than your present life to study as much as you can. Many books have been published, and there are also many well-developed study materials. So, I'm certain that the intellectual level of the people of these times is at the highest of levels. I'm sure that there has never been a time that had such a large mass of intellectual people, such a large group of intelligent people. In this sense, people today have as much knowledge as the gods did when they lived on Earth in ancient times. Or you could say that people are given this chance to have that level of knowledge.

Because we are living in this kind of time, I hope that you will learn the Truths as deeply as possible in the true sense. This is the reason why I have purposefully included the principle of wisdom in the principles of happiness. The principle of wisdom, of course, teaches that to study the knowledge of the Truths should be our starting point. Also, at the same time, it teaches that we shouldn't allow this knowledge to stay at a purely intellectual level. Instead, we should transform this knowledge into wisdom based on our real-life experiences of enlightenment, missionary work, and life in the workplace. It's possible to gain as much knowledge of the Truths as you seek.

I provide various kinds of knowledge that many kinds of people can accept. After all, the knowledge that each of you needs to answer the problems in your workbook of life has a certain inclination. There is a certain disposition that leans toward one side or another. For example, your workbook's problems could be inclined toward the subject of love, while other people may be disposed to have problems in another area. To solve the problems in your workbook of life, you need to make efforts in a certain direction, and that direction is the main area where you will find the knowledge of the Truths that is essential for you.

When you put this knowledge into practice and make it your own wisdom, you will realize, "I see, now, that this is what I needed to do. By doing this, I can break through my problems. By doing this, I can cut the worries from my mind and resolve them." This is, in other words, your small enlightenment. So, please believe that there is no end to the small enlightenments you can attain, and I believe that each and every day, or perhaps once a week or once a month, you will experience enlightenment inside you. It's very important to continue accumulating this kind of enlightenment inside yourself.

Therefore, you will need to have the knowledge of the Truths as your foundation and put them into practice in your real life so they can be transformed into wisdom. Your wisdom itself can guide other people.

When other people are stumbling over the same problems you have faced yourself, you will be able to give them words of enlightenment to help them bounce back. You will be able to do so because you have been through the same kind of suffering yourself. You, too, have suffered through a divorce and persevered to recover from this experience, for example. You learned the Truths and practiced them, and you thought about them, and thought about them, and thought about them. You were then able to realize what you should have done. So, when you encounter others who are going through a similar circumstance in their life, you will be able to talk to them and offer them your support.

Or perhaps you suffered through the failure of your business, but through your encounter with the Truths, you were able to rebuild your life. If so, you can stop people who also failed in their businesses from committing suicide. Your knowledge about money is not only what will help you save these people from taking their own lives. The only people who can save them are those who have been tempered through real-life business experiences, gained knowledge, studied the Truths, learned the truths about the spirit world, and about our lives in this world. Neither a doctor nor a police officer can keep people who are facing business failures from taking their own lives. It's the mission of a religious person, after all. A religious person is needed.

Even if you suffer through something, if you acquire this knowledge and turn it into light within yourself—if you turn it into words of wisdom—then you will be able to guide other people. This is the purpose of learning the Truths.

We're a Religion that Is Open to New Knowledge

This is the reason why it's important to turn your knowledge of the Truths into wisdom. At the same time, our organization remains open to the world of knowledge and information so that we don't become an outdated religion. The principle of wisdom represents this aspect of us. It shows that our religion is not one that focuses on going back to ancient times. Happy Science is a religion that is going to help and save even the people of the future. In this sense, we are a religion that will continue making progress and a religion with a system in place to ensure that we remain intellectually open. We are a religion that will take in one new thing after another, whether it's knowledge or technology, as long as it serves people's happiness. Our religion is open in this way.

Fundamentally, there are unchanging spiritual laws that have existed since ancient times that we cannot change. But the methods of living in this earthly world will see changes, and we will, of course, continue to take in better ways of thinking, better information, and better knowledge as these things arise. We have this kind of openness to the world of knowledge.

This is one of the reasons that we at Happy Science are providing information to modern society and expressing our opinions about the future. I am by no means trying to say that we should go back to the Jomon period*.

Since the Truths are universal, they still hold true today. Wearing the guise of this kind of modern information and knowledge, these Truths that still hold true today will be able to fulfill a new role. The Truths are capable of saving people of these times from their suffering.

The people of the Jomon period may have struggled about how to make good earthenware. But nowadays, people suffer from more advanced problems, so the solutions for ancient times don't apply to modern issues.

Of course, there may be people outside our range of expertise and influence who we just cannot save. But Happy Science's organization is open and we are also eager to acquire new knowledge. This shows that we are not a closed, cult-like religion.

---

* TF: The Jomon period is a prehistoric time in Japan that began around 12,000 years ago and lasted until 2,400 years ago.

We are open to academic knowledge and other various kinds of information, including from the mass media. Usually, when religious organizations become open to this kind of information, it results in the organization's demise. This is the reason why other religious organizations don't let this kind of knowledge into their organizations; they keep themselves closed off.

But we incorporate them to some degree, and this is because we have confidence in ourselves, and if we ever notice something wrong, we would like to change it. In this way, I teach the principle of love as the first wide gateway to the Truths, and it's then followed by the principle of wisdom.

5

The Principle of Self-Reflection

The Power of Self-Reflection to Repair Your Past Mistakes

The third principle is the principle of self-reflection. In Buddhism, they teach the Eightfold Path as a practice of self-reflection. It might be a difficult teaching. But in a simple way, many of us have learned about self-reflection in the moral sense. When you did something wrong when you were small, your parents probably reprimanded you and told you to think about what you had done wrong.

But actually, the practice of self-reflection is tremendously connected to our sense of the world. In other words, the practice of self-reflection is a law of physics that runs through the world of the Truths, which is a world that spans from this earthly world to the spirit world. This means that self-reflection differentiates these worlds. As long as we are human beings living in this world, we are blind and have many things we do not understand. So, we make many mistakes.

This is something that God and the *bodhisattvas* understand very well. They know that if they were to be born into this world as us, they too would make mistakes. They understand very well that they too would fumble blindly through this world. So, they have a deep mind of compassion about this aspect of human life.

As human beings, we inevitably make mistakes, and we have been given the freedom to do so. But our mistakes are forgiven because we are also capable of repairing them. We are prone to making mistakes, but we were also created with the ability to reflect on them. Because we have the ability to practice self-reflection, we are able to undo our mistakes.

We may no longer be able to do anything to change what has already happened in the earthly sense or matters regarding the physical body. But you can undo them regarding the facts of the world of your mind because the world of the mind runs through the past, present, and future. With irreparable things, there's no sense in practicing self-reflection. There are things in this world that are irreparable, such as a broken flower vase. No matter how much self-reflection you practice, it cannot be repaired fully.

But when we self-reflect deeply within our mind on our sins from wrongful deeds and trace them back in time, they can be made to vanish. Many bad facts and thoughts are written within our minds and recorded on our thought tape in red words. But when you look back on your life since when you were born and reflect on yourself in light of the Truths, you will come to moments when you say to yourself, "It was wrong of me to do that. I should have taken this other way, instead. I will make sure to never commit this mistake again. I won't sow bad seeds like this one anymore." When you practice self-reflection in this way, the red words recorded in your mind do not turn into words written in black, but in gold. This is the outcome of self-reflection.

Therefore, there are many things in this material world which aren't reparable, but what has happened within our own minds can be repaired. It's for this purpose that we are given the practice of self-reflection. Even if it's something that occurred in the past, we are still able to self-reflect on it and repair it. By self-reflecting with an honest heart, we can go through all of our wrongs and make them vanish as if we were going over them with a white-out pen. We were given this great power to do so.

If you feel that you have committed so many wrongs that you're a miserable person, this thought that you are miserable is the starting point. You can start your self-reflective training from this point and change yourself. When you do and you reach enough depth in your self-reflection, the wrongs of your past will become erased.

I once talked about the story of Angulimala in the first chapter of *The Laws of Great Enlightenment**. In a location one or two kilometers (approximately 1 mile) from one of Shakyamuni Buddha's largest religious bases in India, the Jetavana Monastery, you can find the burial mound of Angulimala. Among the burial mounds of other Shakyamuni Buddha's disciples, his is the

---

* TF: See Ryuho Okawa, *The Laws of Great Enlightenment* (New York: IRH Press, 2019).

largest of all. It's the largest one and is located near the Jetavana Monastery.

Angulimala was a monster who is said to have killed a hundred or a thousand people. But he repented of his sins and entered the order of Shakyamuni Buddha's disciples. He had stones thrown at him when he went to collect alms from the people, and he went through spiritual training in this way. When people saw this sinful man repent for his wrongdoings and put his blood and sweat into becoming a bodhisattva of light, their hearts were struck. This is the reason why a large burial mound had been built in tribute to a once blood-thirsty killer, and it exists even today, 2,500 years later.

I believe that this shows that people recognized that converting from evil, as he did, has great power to save people. It might be true that someone pure, righteous, and splendid, who has not a spot of wrong within them, is able to save many people. But someone who has committed many wrongs but has then self-reflected, made great efforts, and rebuilt his or her life also has great power to guide people. Buddhism recognizes this. Nothing in Buddhism has ever said that you cannot be saved if you commit even one act of evil. Instead, Buddhism teaches that if you convert your mind and enter the path of enlightenment, you may be able to gain far greater power than if you haven't had committed such a wrong. It teaches that it's possible to shine with this kind of much greater guiding light. Please know that there is this sort of power in self-reflection. There is also prayer, of course. There are prayers about the future.

There are righteous prayers to help you change your future. It's my hope that you will practice and experience this mystical aspect of the mind.

Experience the Refreshing
Feeling of Evil Spirits Coming Off of You

You will see how much power you will get from self-reflection. When you do, I think that some of you will feel the evil spirit that had been possessing you for many years peel away. Since they are spirits, we may tend to believe that they don't have any weight, but they actually feel heavy. So, even though it's said that our spirit body doesn't physically weigh anything, there is a heaviness that you feel in the spiritual sense. The spirits have probably been possessing you for five, ten, or twenty years. You may have gotten them from your own family, perhaps your parents. There may be ones you've been bearing the burden of since your childhood.

When you practice self-reflection, this heaviness can be taken away. When it is, you will feel the burden lift from your shoulders, hips, and back. All of a sudden, you will feel much better, as if a burden had been lifted off you. It truly, suddenly goes away, and you will feel much lighter. A flush will return to your cheeks, and a feeling of warm sunshine will pour into your heart. I truly hope that you will get to experience this feeling. It's a spiritual experience that anyone can attain.

People who have struggled and struggled and suffered and suffered and then finally come upon the Truths have also probably experienced possession by evil spirits, and they may still be under such disturbances. Unless these spiritual beings exist around you, there won't be so much suffering for you. Having this suffering in real life means that something attached to you is coming to you nightly to make you anguish. It's trying hard to drag you down to hell, delighting in driving your mind into anguish. There are spirits coming to you with this kind of evil intention. When you're able to make them go away, you will feel the sense of relief of having just come from taking a bath, fresh and clear of mind, a pink flush glowing upon your face, and a weightless ease in your heart. You will feel your whole body become lighter. It will feel as though 10 years have gone by without a bath and now you have washed off the grime that had been accumulating on your skin. This is the way it will feel. It's a feeling of warm sunshine inside yourself.

This is a harmless spiritual experience that I hope you'll get to experience if you can. This experience may come to you while you are practicing self-reflection, or it may also, of course, come to you while you are reading one of my books. It may come to you during a ritual prayer for expelling evil disturbances, Zen, another kind of meditation, or during religious rituals at the local temples or shojas of Happy Science. Then, evil spirits will lift right off you, and you will feel lighter. I don't know when this will happen to you, but as long as you keep on joining Happy Science's activities, the chance for you to experience this is certain to come.

Based on my thorough knowledge of this, I put together the outline of my teachings, various religious rituals, and also have instructed the lecturers. We conduct these things based on a good understanding of such things that happen in reality, so a turning point will surely arrive someday to bring a change to your life.

If an evil disturbance is possessing you, this disturbance first needs to be removed. Otherwise, you will not be able to hear the words of your guardian spirit, even if they're trying to communicate with you. You're basically in a state of covering your ears to their words, so you won't be able to listen to their opinions.

This is why some people, even though they've been introduced to the Truths and have read my books, are unable to come to the local temples, the headquarters, or the shojas. They are unable to enter them. Various things happen to obstruct them from going. Their families might get into accidents or might oppose their wishes. They might say this thing and that thing and turn around just as they are reaching Happy Science. Many believers probably have had these types of experiences.

Afraid that it will be their end if the person they're possessing sets foot into Happy Science, they try to stop the person from entering our doors. If he or she decides to believe in Happy

Science's teachings, the disruptions the evil spirits have been causing will become apparent and they won't be able to remain attached. If he or she receives a *Home Gohonzon*, an object of worship, it's basically the same as the evil spirits being watched over every single day. They cannot bear having *The True Words Spoken by Buddha* recited in front of the Gohonzon. It feels to them as if they are being preached to every day. So, they wonder whether the person will keep doing this forever till the end of their life, and so the evil spirits' true feelings say, "I don't want to spend much more time with this person."

This is the reason why making spiritual training a habit is very important in any religion. It's not enough to practice it once in a while. If you recite *The True Words Spoken by Buddha* and practice self-reflection in front of the Gohonzon every day, day and night, the light will begin to shine from you, and the evil spirit will not be able to help but go away from you eventually. There will come a turning point when the spiritual possession ends. It will come off little by little, but a point will arrive when it will come off you fully and won't be able to become attached to you again.

In the beginning, the evil spirit will attach itself and then go away and it will continue to do this, back and forth. It will try to cause disturbances for you and create trouble. For example, if you become a member and your spouse is against your coming to Happy Science, the spiritual disturbance attached to you might transfer to your spouse and influence him or her to tell you not to come to our local temples or join our activities. Your spouse may tell you that it's more important to take care of the backyard on Sundays and do other chores to keep you from going to the local temple. If you experience a case like this, it wouldn't be wrong to think that the evil disturbance has transferred from you to your spouse. Eventually, its influence will weaken.

After the evil spirit has left you completely, try to spread the teachings to your spouse or your children next, which will strengthen the spiritual light around you. If you do this, the evil disturbance will not be able to stay with you any longer.

This is the work I am doing. Even though it cannot be recognized visibly, this is what I do day in and day out, throughout the country. I work all throughout the year, 365 days a year, without rest. I have been doing this continually for a very long time. I have been giving out light continually, throughout the year, for there are no rest days in the world of God. I have never rested. I have continually been fighting. The fight with evil spirits will continue.

So, please, believe in me. When people believe in me, the light will shine from them and they will fight the evil disturbances.

Evil spirits are also suffering beings since they were also human beings once. It's important that we stop them from committing further evil deeds and that we make them self-reflect, too. Please self-reflect on yourself. I hope that when the evil spirits see others self-reflecting and shining with light, they will also reflect on themselves. This is one of the things that I'm hoping will occur and something I would like to gradually accomplish.

6

The Principle of Progress

A Happiness that Can Be Brought from This World to the Other World

Fourthly, there is the principle of progress. I gave this teaching as one for this modern age. In Buddhist terms, this is the creation of a Buddhaland utopia, a God's utopia. In the earthly sense of the word, I hope that people who learn the Truths will become successful, because the power of our impact will grow larger by doing so. I hope people won't become too attached, become overly miserly, crave promotions at work, or become attached to their positions at work. Instead, I hope to see people who have learned the Truths achieve success and gain greater influence over the people around them. I hope that they attain the kind of happiness that they can bring with them from this world to the other world. Since I've given clear teachings on the other world, I don't think that Happy Science believers would ever seek only a worldly happiness.

Also, my teachings don't insist on becoming *un*happy in this world to find happiness in the other world. I am not teaching that you should become *un*happy in this earthly world, get a death sentence, or get killed. Other religions may tell you to do these things, but I feel a greater responsibility. I don't wish to sow any new seeds of unhappiness, to the extent that I can avoid it. I would like people to become as happy in this world as is possible for them. If the happiness you attain in this world is not based on taking advantage of others' happiness, it will be of the kind that you can bring with you to the other world. But if your happiness comes from trampling on others, you won't be able to take it with you into your afterlife.

If your happiness comes from making others happier, there's nothing more you could ask for. I would like you to gain this kind of happiness in this world and bring it with you into the afterlife. This is my hope. In this sense, I hope that our lay members will achieve prosperity and progress in their work without having attachments and become a new source of power for our missionary work. I hope that my professional disciples will also feel deeply their own soul's growth, a sense of the success of their own soul.

Creating a World of God on Earth Will Help Shrink the Size of Hell

In addition, I would like to transform this world into God's utopia. When this world becomes a world of God, the size of hell will shrink. We cannot make hell itself disappear that easily by trying to erase it. Instead, we need to begin by cutting off hell's supply stream. To do that, we need to make this world a world of God.

In this way, hell's supply stream will dry up, and the people in hell who self-reflect will gradually come up to heaven from that world. As one and then another gradually get out of hell, the number of people in hell will decrease. Unless we stop hell at its source, if there are new supply sources everywhere, it won't matter how many souls we succeed in saving. Our efforts will only lead to an ongoing cycle that will never end. So, we will need to change this world itself. We will need to change this world into a world of God.

I hope for many people to learn the Truths and explore the right mind, and I hope that everyone will seek the principles of happiness. I would like to change the world in this way.

7

Love, Enlightenment, and the Creation of Utopia

Happy Science's essential teaching is to explore the right mind, and the concrete teaching that will help you do this is the teaching of the principles of happiness—the Fourfold Path. Also, if you look closely, you will see that I have given various teachings that can be summed up into the three themes of love, enlightenment, and the creation of utopia.

When you study my teachings, you can see that I put these three themes of love, enlightenment, and the creation of utopia at the center. I've offered various teachings on love, and when we have strongly emphasized this teaching, we have drawn the interest of people with a Christian leaning. I also have given teachings on how to seek enlightenment, and when I have, I have drawn the interest of people with a Buddhist leaning. Then, when I have strongly emphasized my teachings on the creation of utopia on Earth, we have drawn modern businesspeople, people wishing to improve their families, and people seeking to attain happiness in society. This is the way things have been.

I would like to achieve victory by creating a body of teachings so vast that it will embrace everything, from the new things that are constantly arising to the old and the things of the future.

I hope that this chapter has provided you with a modern introduction to Happy Science.

CHAPTER FIVE

BELIEVING THE AGE OF THE SUN WILL COME

The Future Society Led by *The Laws of the Sun*

1

What the Age of the Sun Will Be Like

In my book *The Laws of the Sun*, which I wrote at the start of Happy Science, I set down the leading principles of our organization. I believe that since the outset of Happy Science, this single book has indicated all our organization's outline, height, and direction. My hope is that this essential book among our essential books will be read deeply and become widely known by as many people as possible. I also hope to see it continually read by the people of today and of the ages to come as the sacred scriptures of the future.

When these Truths, these values, told by *The Laws of the Sun* spread throughout the world and become leading values, I would like the future society that will appear to be called the Age of the Sun. Long ago, these were also Truths taught in a different shape in the Land of Mu, which prospered in the South Pacific Ocean.

2

A World with a Backbone of Faith

The Eyes of the Original God, Our Creator

There is the splendid sun. What spiritual Laws does the sun symbolize? What are the Truth-based values that shine like the sun upon humanity? There are several points that could sum them up.

What is most important is our wish to create a country and a world based on the singular backbone of faith. In these times now, the world is in a highly advanced age of materialism and convenience. This convenience is something I do not have any intention of denying. I also don't intend to propose returning to primitive times. But there is something that we shouldn't forget in this civilization of convenience and materialism, and that something is faith. When the central principles of the universe are forgotten and we live in the name of trifles, we lose our direction and fall into committing mistakes. One or two people could be forgiven, but when many people are straying in the wrong direction, a mighty reaction will eventually come.

To avert hundreds of millions or billions of people from a great mistake in the great flow of the world, what's fundamentally essential is people's faith. No matter how far we gaze into this universe, we see only empty space dotted by small shining stars. But this space is not without living beings. There are living organisms that live in this universe. And there is also a great being watching compassionately over everyone.

It's exactly as I've described in *The Laws of the Sun* about the history of the creation of the universe. There appeared in the beginning the Will. The Will appeared, saying, "Let there be." The Big Bang could not have appeared materially without this Will that existed first. The resulting physical phenomenon can be explained in various ways, but the Will was there at the onset.

It was by dint of this Will that the phenomenal world came into creation. When this Will gathered itself into a single, focused point, it materialized physically and manifested itself into this world. Just as there cannot be a child without parents, the universe could not have been created without a Will. It was due to this Will and its desire to nurture evolving, living beings that our universe came into creation.

It can be said that this parental heart belongs to the Original God. It is a gaze from a world at an eternally far off distance. To the human eye, this third-dimensional universe appears to extend on and on infinitely, but to the eyes of the Original God, this universe appears very small, like a droplet of water. Such are the eyes with which this being looks upon us.

Believe in this truth. And believe that for the sake of continually conveying His Will, the Original God brought many guiding spirits and angels of light into creation and has been continuing to guide a great many of humankind and living beings. This belief is essential to you to avoid heading in the wrong direction.

This World and the Other World Mutually Influence Each Other

However advanced science and technology have become, there is a line that cannot be crossed. This line represents the very principles of the Universe, which cannot be changed. We human beings can do all we can to invent and devise things, but nothing we do can ever change these principles themselves, because they were created of the original Will.

I am referring not only to the laws of physics that run through third-dimensional space but also to the principles that run through the earthly lives that we human beings live. These principles say that we human beings don't just live inside physical bodies; we also have true homes in the world beyond this world, and we were born to this world for the training of our souls.

It's not a principle that is only true for human beings. It also holds true for animal and plant beings. Flowering plants live in the world beyond this one, including some that have not existed in this earthly world since ancient times. Extinct animals also continue to live in the world beyond this one. This is the true world.

This is a governing principle that we cannot change. From the standpoint of this material world and the world of highly advanced science, it might seem beyond your comprehension, at first glance, and you might not have learned about it in your school education. But just not knowing about something does not mean that this something doesn't exist. Whatever exists, exists. It exists without question.

You are living in this doubly structured world, something you must not forget. To add to that, this world and the other world are not separate places but are layered worlds that influence each other.

Nowadays, people have been debating whether the existence of the other world can be proven medically through near-death experiences. Some say that so many of the worlds reported through near-death experiences have splendidly blooming grass and flower fields, and because of this, these scenes must only be the result of physical reactions in the person's brain. They think that if the other world truly existed, there wouldn't be reports of such ancient places and that because there have never been reports of modern scenery, the other world must not exist.

It's mistaken to think in this way. Just as this earthly world changes, the other world goes through changes too. When modern people pass away from this world, they will find the same lifestyles as their lives in this earthly world. Modern people who have been to the other world and come back don't recall ancient worlds from hundreds or thousands of years ago. The other world now is extremely modernized, actually. Heaven and hell have been changing, too, and urban cities have also appeared there.

Through the world of thoughts, almost everything existing in this world has a counterpart there. When many people wish for something to exist, it becomes manifested into reality. This is the way the other world is. When many people wish for automobiles to exist, they appear, and so do trains and airplanes even though metal does not exist in the other world. They still become manifested there.

So, if there are many people wishing for an earthly paradise, a splendid modern theme park or a beautiful park will appear there. They won't look ancient; they'll look exactly as we would find them in the modern world on Earth.

Although some people refuse to believe in the other world because they only hear ancient worlds being talked about in near-death stories this is not the case there. Worlds like this modern earthly world have already begun to appear there.

There are almost no differences in the times between here and there. It's true that there are worlds where time has stopped in long-ago ages. But to those who go back from this modern world, guidance is given to help them in a way they're able to understand. In the other world, there are schools and hospitals that look just the way they do in this world. Many people work in them, and the work they do is continually and steadily changing. In the spirit world of long-ago times, there weren't any foreign students in our schools, but now in the schools of the spirit world, there are many students from other countries. In this way, the other world is changing similarly to how this earthly world is changing.

We are all living in a vast world and going through a very long course of multiple reincarnations. So, we should not think of our lives only in the limited terms of the time and space of this world.

Broaden your perspective. Believe in the Original Being who created even the great universe, including the spirit world. Also, believe in the beings who are guiding people in His stead. Faith like this is where we ought to begin. This should be your foundation. This is where you first must begin. You must truly put your all into spreading these things throughout the world.

But in Japan especially, materialistic forces have rooted themselves so deeply that speaking of the other world and religious belief would invite ridicule from 60 to 70 percent of the people. These are the forces of ignorance that we must also fight against.

This is not a fight we engage in merely for the sake of fighting. It's a fight of love. It's a fight for the Truths. So many people are suffering for much longer periods than they have to, by as much as 10 times longer, because they led mistaken lives due to lacking knowledge of the Truths. The same can be said regarding anything else. If people could know the Truths sooner, they could reduce this suffering.

3

Devote Your Life to God's Love

Change Your Perspective for the Sake of Happiness

How should we human beings live in the Age of the Sun? First, we should have religious faith, and then also, we should live a life of love. The world of love is to be created. These words have been taught since long ago, in the time of Jesus 2,000 years ago, because the heart of love and mercy is fundamental in the great being we call God or sometimes Buddha. This heart has long been giving life to people and guiding them.

As children of God, we human beings are also meant to live for the sake of love and mercy. People tend to misunderstand love because they think of it as something that is taken from others, as often seems to be true in many novels. People think of love as something that brings them happiness when they receive it and unhappiness when they don't. They think of how they can be loved by others, how much love they can get from others, and how much they can get other people to do things for themselves. Many people only think about love in this way, and so this world is filled with people who are craving but empty of people who live in a state of giving. This is the world we see around us. We would live in

THE LAWS of HAPPINESS

happiness if we would only help one another, but we keep taking from each other instead, and there is no happiness to be found in that.

It's a sad state that this world is in. If we could change our perspective, if we could create a change in our mind we can be happy. Love could become something that is not taken but rather given to others. This giving originates in our inner nature as human beings, as children of God.

Your Devotion to God's Love
Proves Your Nature as a Child of God

God lives in love and mercy. This is the reason that living in devotion to God's love proves your nature as a child of God. God's world is a world of only giving. Just as the sun above us doesn't ask a penny for repayment, God gives continually.

Always live with thoughts of benefiting others.
Always give to others.
Imagine continually what you can do for others,
Not what others can do for you.
For when you do, a heaven will appear on Earth.

There are many difficult theories of love. But the most important theory is the simplest. Love is not something to be taken from others. In Buddhist terms, love that takes from others is only an attachment, a latching onto something. Don't *take* love; *give* love. Love is about how much you have done to love others. Love is not about counting how much love you've been deprived of. Instead, love means thinking about how well you have loved others throughout your life up to now and how you will love others from this moment on. This is the driving force to create the forthcoming utopia.

4

Aim for Higher Enlightenment

Your Mind Itself Is the Essence of Your Soul

I have spoken of love as a basic principle. I cannot help but add to this that enlightenment is also an essential principle. Many people may strongly associate the word "enlightenment" with Buddhism, and they may think it's just one kind of religious thinking. But it's vital, regardless. The simple way I would explain enlightenment is that it's to realize that we human beings are not our physical bodies. A soul or mind exists inside the bodies we are living in or controlling.

Some people regard Buddhism as proposing atheism, materialism, or the non-existence of souls. But they don't necessarily believe it teaches that we human beings do not have a mind. Even people who believe that Buddhism teaches egolessness and that if teaches we don't have souls cannot say that human beings don't have minds.

In truth, our mind itself is the essence of our soul. On returning to the other world, our mind is the only thing we can bring with us. Your mistakes arise because you believe that your soul is defined or fixed in this third-dimensional world. But don't you think freely of your own will? Don't you have many thoughts? Buddhism teaches you that only these thoughts of yours will remain and continue to exist in the other world as who you are. It's these thoughts appearing in you. It's the thinking function in you, and only this thinking function returns with you to the other world. Of course, you'll appear in human form in the other world when you still have memories of your life in this world. But as these memories fade away, you'll stop taking on this appearance. Only your thinking and thoughts will continue to exist.

If human beings were only wind-up dolls, we would never have any thoughts. Wind-up dolls only move according to how their mechanism was created. But we are not wind-up dolls in reality. Human beings are capable of various thoughts. We can also choose how we think. We can choose freely, of our own will. We can freely determine our thoughts by ourselves. This power to change and determine your thoughts is your essence. It's the essence of you as a human being, and when your body perishes, your being continues to exist in the other world.

The thinking and thoughts within your mind continue to exist there. Some people today might not accept the concept of the soul, but even the sublime thoughts of long gone people who lived centuries or millennia ago continue to exist in the great spirit world. The thoughts of such people and the soul's light within them have remained in the other world and continue to influence many people even now.

For example, let's say that Jesus Christ lived in this world for 33 years. But the death of his body did not signify the end of his work. His thoughts from his life have continued to pour forth their work and they continue to do so even now. Shakyamuni Buddha left this world 2,500 years ago, during Japan's Jomon period. Some people may wonder how much content the teachings of someone of such an ancient period could have had. But Shakyamuni Buddha's heart of mercy and enlightenment continues to exist even now. This is the mystical fact of the spirit world.

In this way, it's important to think that you are a spiritual being, that you are the mind within you—and further, to know that you are not the mind of delusion, but your mind's deeper essence. This type of change in your sense of self is essential. It's important to look at yourself in this different light, to change how you view yourself. This change in your perspective is vital.

Raising Your Enlightenment
Is a Way of Planning a Better Future

As various teachings say, your mind will rise to a higher level, become purified, and be made to shine brighter as you strive, through your soul training, to grow yourself closer to God. And even while you are living in this world, how much your mind grows accords exactly with the world you will return to in the afterlife. A life led as a bodhisattva will lead you to the world of bodhisattvas when you pass on from this world. You will not be going to a different destination.

Therefore, you can realize whether you are headed to heaven or hell while you still live in this world. If you look at the thoughts going through your mind day after day, year after year, or for a decade, and the quality of those thoughts, you can see what area of the other world should be your dwelling or which part of the other world you originally came from. Therefore, raising your enlightenment is a way of planning a better future to come. It will determine your life's future, and it will also mean your awakening to your life's true mission. This is an extremely important thing.

5

The Creation of Utopia on Earth

God's Great Design

You must cherish the practical principle of "giving love to others" and the principle of self-improvement of "knowing who you are and what your essential nature is." Humankind must take these two great weapons of love and enlightenment and use them to create a utopia in this world.

I don't mean a material utopia. I don't wish at all to deny the conveniences of this world, and I also do not want to deny the importance of food, clothing, shelter, or anything else in and of itself. These things contribute to people's happiness, and I fully understand this.

But we can't mistake the trifles for the essentials. Please don't forget that we are here in this world for the training of our souls. The various worldly benefits of civilization exist to serve as our spiritual training in this world. It's important that we don't confuse these essentials with trifles. And it's essential that we build a society of the heart that allows everyone to seek love and enlightenment in their lives, whatever shape each individual person and society may take on.

The utopian world we are seeking does not necessarily take on a visible shape. It is not a world that has a certain kind of building, certain kinds of roads, a certain political philosophy, certain economic principles, or certain ways of life. These things change variously over time.

What's important, instead, is for people to know the direction that never changes, even amid constant change, and to realize that this is the direction to head in. It's essential to know about this sublime reality and to bring this world on Earth close to the world of bodhisattvas, *tathagatas*, and angels. It's for this spiritual discipline that a great number of people spend lengths and lengths of time in this world to undergo training of the soul. This has been God's great design.

Saving Many Others by Spreading the Truths

This kind of story may seem fantastical when looked at from the perspective of what you learned in school and from living in society. But when you depart from this world and journey to the other world, all of you, without exception, will realize that my words have been 100 percent true.

People may say to you, "Since we will find out after we die, can't we just wait for that time to come and see what happens then?" But it's better for each and every person to realize the truth of what I have said, even a single day faster.

I want to help those who are living in this world with me at this time to avoid the fate of spending hundreds of anguishing years in the dark world called hell. We are all living in this world together. We are sharing the same kind of information with one another. And yet, for some reason or another, there are people who make mistakes and commit errors.

There is such a thing as a wrong way of life—there is no mistake about that. It is necessary to teach and lend a hand to these people. This is the work of the angels of heaven, it's true. But it's our duty to also tell them while they are still living in this world.

The great driving force for building a utopia shall come also from the power of missionary work. Missionary work is love. Please don't forget that. Our work to spread the Truths is needed to save numerous people. In this sense, it's necessary to spread the Truths to as many people as possible.

It is my hope that as many people as possible will join us. I feel that the strength of my believers is still weak. When more and more numbers of people become believers, we will reach a tipping point, and the moment will come when the greater part of the world will think of my words as Truths.

I hope that this day will come as soon as possible. I pray that the single book, called *The Laws of the Sun*, will reach as many people as possible and become a guide for those who have yet to encounter the Truths. I pray it will open them to the world of

Truths, let the scales clouding their eyes fall off, and let them begin new lives as children of God.

AFTERWORD

I wonder what kind of impression you received from reading this book. I've given teachings on the Truths from a variety of angles in the past, but this book is the very first one aimed at introducing Happy Science's essential teachings straightforwardly. I am planning to continue to write this series, one book after another. At this point, I anticipate that this eighth book will mark the first turnaround point.

Here, in this book, I have reorganized and reconstructed my basic thinking. That was my true aim. But I believe that this book by itself has the power to save a great many people's hearts.

Shakyamuni Buddha, India's Gautama Siddhartha, taught the Eightfold Path 2,500 years ago, but the people of today find it to be a difficult teaching. It's seen now as something from the faraway past. So, I searched for a new path that's suited and easily understandable to the people of today. This is the reason I teach the principles of happiness—the modern Fourfold Path built upon four pillars.

The first principle on this path is the principle of love, the second is the principle of wisdom, the third is the principle of self-reflection, and the fourth is the principle of progress. In this way, I have indicated a new way to practice. If you are able to devote your life to mastering these four pillars, these four principles, your future in this life and the afterlife will shine abundantly. Love is a simple word, but resurrecting the true meaning of love, the sense of mercy taught by Shakyamuni Buddha, is very difficult in these times. This is what I feel.

In addition, in these times of limitless progress as an information society, I purposefully teach the principle of wisdom as a religious principle. Of course, this principle includes the Truths, which is my true wish. But this principle goes beyond the Truths to include the range of general knowledge available in society. The scope of this principle includes an understanding of the future development of academic knowledge and information that will spread limitlessly. I ask you to clearly recognize the modern quality of this teaching.

The principle of self-reflection goes back to the root principles of a religion; it addresses the things that Buddhism and Christianity sought to teach. For people who would like to learn this principle much more deeply, I recommend reading my other books or taking a seminar at Happy Science.

The modern and future-oriented quality of the principle of progress may surprise you, and you may wonder, "Is this truly something being taught by a religion?" This itself is one of the characteristic qualities of Happy Science. In addition, this principle is not just future-oriented, but also takes on the perspective of a Greek spirit of mind to teach the path of building a utopia in this world, which is what we human beings should live for. We can even say that this principle is pointing out what Buddhism, Christianity, and Islam, all of which are facing an impasse, should aim to become.

It fills me with relief to put out a book such as this, which I would say is the most basic of the essential books. I will be most happy if it becomes a book that many people will learn from.

Next, I am planning to publish the ninth book of the Laws Series, *The Mystical Laws**. In this book, I would like to tell you the truths about the limitless mystical spiritual world. If you can wait for one year, I hope you will enjoy it.

Ryuho Okawa
Master and CEO of Happy Science Group
December 2003

---

* TF: The English version is available. See Ryuho Okawa, *The Mystical Laws* (Tokyo: HS Press, 2015).

*This book is a compilation of the lectures
as listed below.*

- CHAPTER ONE -

HOW NOT TO BE UNHAPPY

Japanese title: *Fuko dearu Koto wo Yameru niwa*

Lecture given on May 27, 2001

- CHAPTER TWO -

ONE STEP UP IN YOUR WORK CAPABILITY

Japanese title: *One Point Up no Shigoto Jutsu*

Lecture given on April 27, 1997

- CHAPTER THREE -

THE FOUR PRINCIPLES OF HUMAN HAPPINESS

Japanese title: *Ningen wo Kofuku ni Suru Yottsu no Genri*

Lecture given on January 2, 2000

- CHAPTER FOUR -

INTRODUCTION TO HAPPY SCIENCE

Japanese title: *Kofuku no Kagaku Nyumon*

Lecture given on December 7, 2003

- CHAPTER FIVE -

BELIEVING THE AGE OF THE SUN WILL COME

Japanese title: *Taiyo no Jidai no Torai wo Shinjite*

Lecture given on July 2, 2000

ABOUT THE AUTHOR

RYUHO OKAWA was born on July 7th 1956, in Tokushima, Japan. After graduating from the University of Tokyo with a law degree, he joined a Tokyo-based trading house. While working at its New York headquarters, he studied international finance at the Graduate Center of the City University of New York. In 1981, he attained Great Enlightenment and became aware that he is El Cantare with a mission to bring salvation to all of humankind. In 1986 he established Happy Science. It now has members in over 100 countries across the world, with more than 700 local branches and temples as well as 10,000 missionary houses around the world. The total number of lectures has exceeded 3,150 (of which more than 150 are in English) and over 2,700 books (of which more than 550 are Spiritual Interview Series) have been published, many of which are translated into 31 languages. Many of the books, including *The Laws of the Sun* have become best sellers or million sellers. To date, Happy Science has produced 20 movies. The original story and original concept were given by the Executive Producer Ryuho Okawa. Recent movie titles are *The Real Exorcist* (live-action, May 2020), *Living in the Age of Miracles* (documentary scheduled to be released in Aug. 2020), and *Twiceborn* (live-action, scheduled to be released in Oct. 2020). He has also composed the lyrics and music of over 100 songs, such as theme songs and featured songs of movies. Moreover, he is the Founder of Happy Science University and Happy Science Academy (Junior and Senior High School), Founder and President of the Happiness Realization Party, Founder and Honorary Headmaster of Happy Science Institute of Government and Management, Founder of IRH Press Co., Ltd., and the Chairperson of New Star Production Co., Ltd. and ARI Production Co., Ltd.

WHAT IS EL CANTARE?

El Cantare means "the Light of the Earth," and is the Supreme God of the Earth who has been guiding humankind since the beginning of Genesis. He is whom Jesus called Father and Muhammad called Allah. Different parts of El Cantare's core consciousness have descended to Earth in the past, once as Alpha and another as Elohim. His branch spirits, such as Shakyamuni Buddha and Hermes, have descended to Earth many times and helped to flourish many civilizations. To unite various religions and to integrate various fields of study in order to build a new civilization on Earth, a part of the core consciousness has descended to Earth as Master Ryuho Okawa.

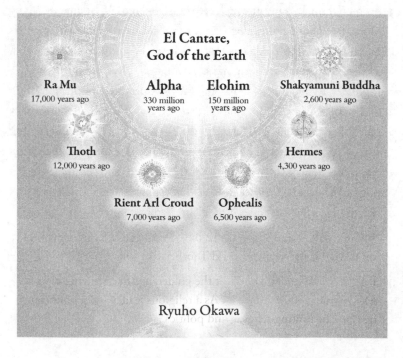

**El Cantare,
God of the Earth**

Ra Mu
17,000 years ago

Alpha
330 million
years ago

Elohim
150 million
years ago

Shakyamuni Buddha
2,600 years ago

Thoth
12,000 years ago

Hermes
4,300 years ago

Rient Arl Croud
7,000 years ago

Ophealis
6,500 years ago

Ryuho Okawa

Alpha is a part of the core consciousness of El Cantare who descended to Earth around 330 million years ago. Alpha preached Earth's Truths to harmonize and unify Earth-born humans and space people who came from other planets.

Elohim is a part of El Cantare's core consciousness who descended to Earth around 150 million years ago. He gave wisdom, mainly on the differences of light and darkness, good and evil.

Shakyamuni Buddha was born as a prince into the Shakya Clan in India around 2,600 years ago. When he was 29 years old, he renounced the world and sought enlightenment. He later attained Great Enlightenment and founded Buddhism.

Hermes is one of the 12 Olympian gods in Greek mythology, but the spiritual Truth is that he taught the teachings of love and progress around 4,300 years ago that became the origin of the current Western civilization. He is a hero that truly existed.

Ophealis was born in Greece around 6,500 years ago and was the leader who took an expedition to as far as Egypt. He is the God of miracles, prosperity, and arts, and is known as Osiris in the Egyptian mythology.

Rient Arl Croud was born as a king of the ancient Incan Empire around 7,000 years ago and taught about the mysteries of the mind. In the heavenly world, he is responsible for the interactions that take place between various planets.

Thoth was an almighty leader who built the golden age of the Atlantic civilization around 12,000 years ago. In the Egyptian mythology, he is known as god Thoth.

Ra Mu was a leader who built the golden age of the civilization of Mu around 17,000 years ago. As a religious leader and a politician, he ruled by uniting religion and politics.

WHAT IS A SPIRITUAL MESSAGE?

We are all spiritual beings living on this earth. The following is the mechanism behind Master Ryuho Okawa's spiritual messages.

1 You are a spirit

People are born into this world to gain wisdom through various experiences and return to the other world when their lives end. We are all spirits and repeat this cycle in order to refine our souls.

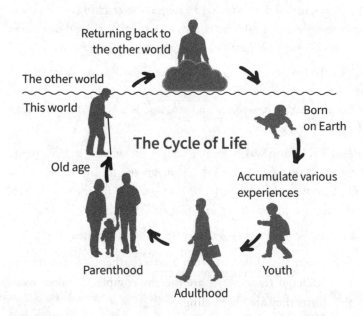

Returning back to the other world

The other world

This world

Born on Earth

The Cycle of Life

Old age

Accumulate various experiences

Parenthood

Adulthood

Youth

2 You have a guardian spirit

Guardian spirits are those who protect the people who are living on this earth. Each of us has a guardian spirit that watches over us and guides us from the other world. They were us in our past life, and are identical in how we think.

The other world

Guardian Spirit

This world

Watches over us/
sends us inspiration

You

3 How spiritual messages work

Master Ryuho Okawa, through his enlightenment, is capable of summoning any spirit from anywhere in the world, including the spirit world.

Master Okawa's way of receiving spiritual messages is fundamentally different from that of other psychic mediums who undergo trances and are thereby completely taken over by the spirits they are channeling.

Master Okawa's attainment of a high level of enlightenment enables him to retain full control of his consciousness and body throughout the duration of the spiritual message. To allow the spirits to express their own thoughts and personalities freely, however, Master Okawa usually softens the dominancy of his consciousness. This way, he is able to keep his own philosophies out of the way and ensure that the spiritual messages are pure expressions of the spirits he is channeling.

Since guardian spirits think at the same subconscious level as the person living on earth, Master Okawa can summon the spirit and find out what the person on earth is actually thinking. If the person has already returned to the other world, the spirit can give messages to the people living on earth through Master Okawa.

Since 2009, more than 1,050 sessions of spiritual messages have been openly recorded by Master Okawa, and the majority of these have been published. Spiritual messages from the guardian spirits of people living today such as Donald Trump, Japanese Prime Minister Shinzo Abe and Chinese President Xi Jinping, as well as spiritual messages sent from the spirit world by Jesus Christ, Muhammad, Thomas Edison, Mother Teresa, Steve Jobs and Nelson Mandela are just a tiny pack of spiritual messages that were published so far.

Domestically, in Japan, these spiritual messages are being read by a wide range of politicians and mass media, and the high-level contents of these books are delivering an impact even more on politics, news and public opinion. In recent years, there have been spiritual messages recorded in English, and English translations are being done on the spiritual messages given in Japanese. These have been published overseas, one after another, and have started to shake the world.

1 The guardian spirit / spirit in the other world...

2 Goes inside Master Okawa in this world

3 Master Okawa speaks the words of the guardian spirit / spirit

*For more about spiritual messages and a complete list of books in the Spiritual Interview Series, visit **okawabooks.com***

ABOUT HAPPY SCIENCE

Happy Science is a global movement that empowers individuals to find purpose and spiritual happiness and to share that happiness with their families, societies, and the world. With more than twelve million members around the world, Happy Science aims to increase awareness of spiritual truths and expand our capacity for love, compassion, and joy so that together we can create the kind of world we all wish to live in.

Activities at Happy Science are based on the principles of happiness (love, wisdom, self-reflection, and progress). These principles embrace worldwide philosophies and beliefs, transcending boundaries of culture and religions.

Love teaches us to give ourselves freely without expecting anything in return; it encompasses giving, nurturing, and forgiving.

Wisdom leads us to the insights of spiritual truths, and opens us to the true meaning of life and the will of God (the universe, the highest power, Buddha).

Self-Reflection brings a mindful, nonjudgmental lens to our thoughts and actions to help us find our truest selves—the essence of our souls—and deepen our connection to the highest power. It helps us attain a clean and peaceful mind and leads us to the right life path.

Progress emphasizes the positive, dynamic aspects of our spiritual growth—actions we can take to manifest and spread happiness around the world. It's a path that not only expands our soul growth, but also furthers the collective potential of the world we live in.

PROGRAMS AND EVENTS

The doors of Happy Science are open to all. We offer a variety of programs and events, including self-exploration and self-growth programs, spiritual seminars, meditation and contemplation sessions, study groups, and book events.

Our programs are designed to:
* Deepen your understanding of your purpose and meaning in life
* Improve your relationships and increase your capacity to love unconditionally
* Attain peace of mind, decrease anxiety and stress, and feel positive
* Gain deeper insights and a broader perspective on the world
* Learn how to overcome life's challenges
  ... and much more.

*For more information, visit **happy-science.org**.*

INTERNATIONAL SEMINARS

Each year, friends from all over the world join our international seminars, held at our faith centers in Japan. Different programs are offered each year and cover a wide variety of topics, including improving relationships, practicing the Eightfold Path to enlightenment, and loving yourself, to name just a few.

HAPPY SCIENCE MONTHLY

Happy Science regularly publishes various magazines for readers around the world. The Happy Science Monthly, which now spans over 300 issues, contains Master Okawa's latest lectures, words of wisdom, stories of remarkable life-changing experiences, world news, and much more to guide members and their friends to a happier life. This is available in many other languages, including Portuguese, Spanish, French, German, Chinese, and Korean. Happy Science Basics, on the other hand, is a 'theme-based' booklet made in an easy-to-read style for those new to Happy Science, which is also ideal to give to friends and family. You can pick up the latest issues from Happy Science, subscribe to have them delivered (see our contacts page) or view them online.*

* Online editions of the *Happy Science Monthly* and
Happy Science Basics can be viewed at:
info.happy-science.org/category/magazines/

CONTACT INFORMATION

Happy Science is a worldwide organization with faith centers around the globe. For a comprehensive list of centers, visit the worldwide directory at *happy-science.org*. The following are some of the many Happy Science locations:

UNITED STATES AND CANADA

New York
79 Franklin St., New York, NY 10013
Phone: 212-343-7972
Fax: 212-343-7973
Email: ny@happy-science.org
Website: happyscience-na.org

San Francisco
525 Clinton St.
Redwood City, CA 94062
Phone & Fax: 650-363-2777
Email: sf@happy-science.org
Website: happyscience-na.org

New Jersey
725 River Rd, #102B, Edgewater, NJ 07020
Phone: 201-313-0127
Fax: 201-313-0120
Email: nj@happy-science.org
Website: happyscience-na.org

Los Angeles
1590 E. Del Mar Blvd., Pasadena, CA 91106
Phone: 626-395-7775
Fax: 626-395-7776
Email: la@happy-science.org
Website: happyscience-na.org

Florida
5208 8th St., St. Zephyrhills, FL 33542
Phone: 813-715-0000
Fax: 813-715-0010
Email: florida@happy-science.org
Website: happyscience-na.org

Orange County
10231 Slater Ave., #204
Fountain Valley, CA 92708
Phone: 714-745-1140
Email: oc@happy-science.org
Website: happyscience-na.org

Atlanta
1874 Piedmont Ave., NE Suite 360-C
Atlanta, GA 30324
Phone: 404-892-7770
Email: atlanta@happy-science.org
Website: happyscience-na.org

San Diego
7841 Balboa Ave., Suite #202
San Diego, CA 92111
Phone: 619-381-7615
Fax: 626-395-7776
E-mail: sandiego@happy-science.org
Website: happyscience-na.org

Hawaii
Phone: 808-591-9772
Fax: 808-591-9776
Email: hi@happy-science.org
Website: happyscience-na.org

Kauai
3343 Kanakolu Street, Suite 5
Lihue, HI 96766, U.S.A.
Phone: 808-822-7007
Fax: 808-822-6007
Email: kauai-hi@happy-science.org
Website: kauai.happyscience-na.org

Toronto
845 The Queensway
Etobicoke ON M8Z 1N6 Canada
Phone: 1-416-901-3747
Email: toronto@happy-science.org
Website: happy-science.ca

Vancouver
#201-2607 East 49th Avenue
Vancouver, BC, V5S 1J9, Canada
Phone: 1-604-437-7735
Fax: 1-604-437-7764
Email: vancouver@happy-science.org
Website: happy-science.ca

INTERNATIONAL

Tokyo
1-6-7 Togoshi, Shinagawa
Tokyo, 142-0041 Japan
Phone: 81-3-6384-5770
Fax: 81-3-6384-5776
Email: tokyo@happy-science.org
Website: happy-science.org

London
3 Margaret St.
London,W1W 8RE United Kingdom
Phone: 44-20-7323-9255
Fax: 44-20-7323-9344
Email: eu@happy-science.org
Website: happyscience-uk.org

Sydney
516 Pacific Hwy, Lane Cove North,
NSW 2066, Australia
Phone: 61-2-9411-2877
Fax: 61-2-9411-2822
Email: sydney@happy-science.org

Seoul
74, Sadang-ro 27-gil,
Dongjak-gu, Seoul, Korea
Phone: 82-2-3478-8777
Fax: 82-2-3478-9777
Email: korea@happy-science.org
Website: happyscience-korea.org

Brazil Headquarters
Rua. Domingos de Morais 1154,
Vila Mariana, Sao Paulo SP
CEP 04009-002, Brazil
Phone: 55-11-5088-3800
Fax: 55-11-5088-3806
Email: sp@happy-science.org
Website: happyscience.com.br

Jundiai
Rua Congo, 447, Jd. Bonfiglioli
Jundiai-CEP, 13207-340
Phone: 55-11-4587-5952
Email: jundiai@happy-science.org

Taipei
No. 89, Lane 155, Dunhua N. Road
Songshan District, Taipei City 105, Taiwan
Phone: 886-2-2719-9377
Fax: 886-2-2719-5570
Email: taiwan@happy-science.org
Website: happyscience-tw.org

Malaysia
No 22A, Block 2, Jalil Link Jalan Jalil Jaya 2,
Bukit Jalil 57000, Kuala Lumpur, Malaysia
Phone: 60-3-8998-7877
Fax: 60-3-8998-7977
Email: malaysia@happy-science.org
Website: happyscience.org.my

Nepal
Kathmandu Metropolitan City Ward
No. 15,
Ring Road, Kimdol,
Sitapaila Kathmandu, Nepal
Phone: 97-714-272931
Email: nepal@happy-science.org

Uganda
Plot 877 Rubaga Road, Kampala
P.O. Box 34130, Kampala, Uganda
Phone: 256-79-4682-121
Email: uganda@happy-science.org
Website: happyscience-uganda.org

Thailand
19 Soi Sukhumvit 60/1,
Bang Chak, Phra Khanong,
Bangkok, 10260 Thailand
Phone: 66-2-007-1419
Email: bangkok@happy-science.org
Website: happyscience-thai.org

Indonesia
Darmawangsa
Square Lt. 2 No. 225
Jl. Darmawangsa VI & IX
Indonesia
Phone: 021-7278-0756
Email: indonesia@happy-science.org

Philippines Taytay
LGL Bldg, 2nd Floor,
Kadalagaham cor,
Rizal Ave. Taytay,
Rizal, Philippines
Phone: 63-2-5710686
Email: philippines@happy-science.org

SOCIAL CONTRIBUTIONS

Happy Science tackles social issues such as suicide and bullying, and launches heartfelt, precise and prompt rescue operations after a major disaster.

◆ The HS Nelson Mandela Fund

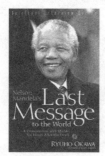

The Happy Science Group provides disaster relief and educational aid overseas via this Fund. We established it following the publication of *Nelson Mandela's Last Message to the World*, a spiritual message from the late Nelson Mandela, in 2013. The fund actively provides both material and spiritual aid to people overseas—support for victims of racial discrimination, poverty, political oppression, natural disasters, and more.

Examples of how the fund has been used:

Provided tents in rural Nepal

Supplied food and water immediately after the Nepal earthquake

Donated a container library to South African primary school, in collaboration with Nelson Mandela Foundation

◆ **We extend a helping hand around the world to aid in post-disaster reconstruction and education.**

NEPAL: From 2015 to 2020 after the Nepal Earthquake, we promptly changed our local temple into a temporary evacuation center and utilized our global network to send water, food and tents. We still keep supporting the rebuilding of schools.

SRI LANKA: Provided aid in constructing school buildings damaged by the tsunami. Further, with the help of the Sri Lankan prime minister, 100 bookshelves were donated to Buddhist temples.

INDIA: Ongoing aid since 2006—uniforms, school meals, etc. for schools in Bodh Gaya, a sacred ground for Buddhism. Medical aid in Kolkata, in collaboration with local hospitals.

CHINA: Donated money and tents to the Szechuan Earthquake disaster zone. Books were also donated to elementary schools in Gansu Province, near the disaster zone.

UGANDA: Donated educational materials and mosquito nets to protect children from Malaria. Donated a school building and prayer hall to a private secondary school, as well as offering a scholarship to a university student who had graduated from the school.

GHANA: Provided medical supplies as a preventive measure against Ebola.

SOUTH AFRICA: Collaborated with the Nelson Mandela Foundation in South Africa to donate a container library and books to an elementary school.

IRAN: Donated to the earthquake-stricken area in northeastern Iran in October 2012, and donated 15,000 masks as medical aid in May 2020 via the Iranian Embassy.

HAPPINESS REALIZATION PARTY

The Happiness Realization Party (HRP) was founded in May 2009 by Master Ryuho Okawa as part of the Happy Science Group to offer concrete and proactive solutions to the current issues such as military threats from North Korea and China and the long-term economic recession. HRP aims to implement drastic reforms of the Japanese government, thereby bringing peace and prosperity to Japan. To accomplish this, HRP proposes two key policies:

1) Strengthening the national security and the Japan-U.S. alliance which plays a vital role in the stability of Asia.

2) Improving the Japanese economy by implementing drastic tax cuts, taking monetary easing measures and creating new major industries.

HRP advocates that Japan should offer a model of a religious nation that allows diverse values and beliefs to coexist, and that contributes to global peace.

*For more information, visit **en.hr-party.jp***

HAPPY SCIENCE ACADEMY
JUNIOR AND SENIOR HIGH SCHOOL

Happy Science Academy Junior and Senior High School is a boarding school founded with the goal of educating the future leaders of the world who can have a big vision, persevere, and take on new challenges.

Currently, there are two campuses in Japan; the Nasu Main Campus in Tochigi Prefecture, founded in 2010, and the Kansai Campus in Shiga Prefecture, founded in 2013.

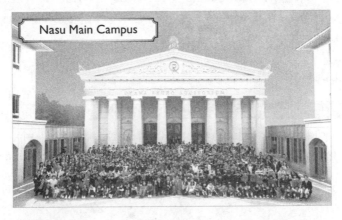

Nasu Main Campus

Kansai Campus

HAPPY SCIENCE UNIVERSITY

THE FOUNDING SPIRIT AND THE GOAL OF EDUCATION

Based on the founding philosophy of the university, "Exploration of happiness and the creation of a new civilization," education, research and studies will be provided to help students acquire deep understanding grounded in religious belief and advanced expertise with the objectives of producing "great talents of virtue" who can contribute in a broad-ranging way to serve Japan and the international society.

FACULTIES

Faculty of Human Happiness

Students in this faculty will pursue liberal arts from various perspectives with a multidisciplinary approach, explore and envision an ideal state of human beings and society.

Faculty of Successful Management

This faculty aims to realize successful management that helps organizations to create value and wealth for society and to contribute to the happiness and the development of management and employees as well as society as a whole.

Faculty of Future Creation

Students in this faculty study subjects such as political science, journalism, performing arts and artistic expression, and explore and present new political and cultural models based on truth, goodness and beauty.

Faculty of Future Industry

This faculty aims to nurture engineers who can resolve various issues facing modern civilization from a technological standpoint and contribute to the creation of new industries of the future.

LIVING IN THE AGE OF
MIRACLES

A documentary film to be released in Aug. 2020

An inspirational documentary about two Japanese actors meeting people who experienced miracles in their lives. Through their quest, they find the key to working miracles and learn what "living in the age of miracles" truly means.

GOLD AWARD
Documentary Feature
International
Independent Film Awards
Spring 2020

GOLD AWARD
Concept
International
Independent Film Awards
Spring 2020

THE REAL EXORCIST

46 Awards from 7 Countries!

STORY Tokyo —the most mystical city in the world where you find spiritual spots in the most unexpected places. Sayuri works as a part time waitress at a small coffee shop "Extra" where regular customers enjoy the authentic coffee that the owner brews. Meanwhile, Sayuri uses her supernatural powers to help those who are troubled by spiritual phenomena one after another. Through her special consultations, she touches the hearts of the people and helps them by showing the truths of the invisible world.

USA

GOLD REMI AWARD
53rd WorldFest Houston
International Film Festival 2020

MONACO
BEST FEATURE FILM
17th Angel Film Awards
2020
Monaco International Film Festival

NIGERIA

BEST FEATURE FILM
EKO International Film Festival
2020

BEST FEMALE ACTOR
17th Angel Film Awards
2020
Monaco International Film Festival

BEST FEMALE SUPPORTING ACTOR
17th Angel Film Awards
2020
Monaco International Film Festival

BEST SUPPORTING ACTRESS
EKO International Film Festival
2020

BEST VISUAL EFFECTS
17th Angel Film Awards
2020
Monaco International Film Festival

...and more!

For more information, visit www.realexorcistmovie.com

ABOUT IRH PRESS USA

IRH Press USA Inc. was founded in 2013 as an affiliated firm of IRH Press Co., Ltd. Based in New York, the press publishes books in various categories including spirituality, religion, and self-improvement and publishes books by Ryuho Okawa, the author of over 100 million books sold worldwide. For more information, visit *okawabooks.com*.

Follow us on:

Facebook: Okawa Books   **Twitter:** Okawa Books

Goodreads: Ryuho Okawa   **Instagram:** OkawaBooks

Pinterest: Okawa Books

RYUHO OKAWA'S LAWS SERIES

The Laws Series is an annual volume of books that are mainly comprised of Ryuho Okawa's lectures on various topics that highlight principles and guidelines for the activities of Happy Science every year. *The Laws of the Sun*, the first publication of the Laws Series, ranked in the annual best-selling list in Japan in 1987. Since then, all of the Laws Series' titles have ranked in the annual best-selling list for more than two decades, setting socio-cultural trends in Japan and around the world.

THE TRILOGY

The first three volumes of the Laws Series, *The Laws of the Sun, The Golden Laws,* and *The Nine Dimensions* make a trilogy that completes the basic framework of the teachings of God's Truths. *The Laws of the Sun* discusses the structure of God's Laws, *The Golden Laws* expounds on the doctrine of time, and *The Nine Dimensions* reveals the nature of space.

BOOKS BY RYUHO OKAWA

The 26th
Laws Series

THE LAWS OF STEEL
LIVING A LIFE OF RESILIENCE, CONFIDENCE AND PROSPERITY

Paperback • 256 pages • $16.95
ISBN: 978-1-942125-65-5

This book is a compilation of six lectures that Ryuho Okawa gave in 2018 and 2019, each containing passionate messages for us to open a brighter future. This powerful and inspiring book will not only show us the ways to achieve true happiness and prosperity, but also the ways to solve many global issues we now face. It presents us with wisdom that is based on a spiritual perspective, and a new design for our future society. Through this book, we can overcome differences in values and create a peaceful world, thereby ushering in a Golden Age.

Chapter list
1 The Mindset to Invite Prosperity
2 The Law of Cause and Effect
3 Fulfilling *Noblesse Oblige*
4 Be Confident in Your Life
5 A Savior's Wish
6 The Power to Make Miracles

---

*For a complete list of books, visit **okawabooks.com***

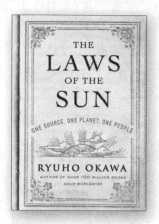

THE LAWS OF THE SUN

ONE SOURCE, ONE PLANET, ONE PEOPLE

Paperback • 288 pages • $15.95
ISBN: 978-1-942125-43-3

IMAGINE IF YOU COULD ASK GOD why He created this world and what spiritual laws He used to shape us—and everything around us. If we could understand His designs and intentions, we could discover what our goals in life should be and whether our actions move us closer to those goals or farther away.

At a young age, a spiritual calling prompted Ryuho Okawa to outline what he innately understood to be universal truths for all humankind. In *The Laws of the Sun*, Okawa outlines these laws of the universe and provides a road map for living one's life with greater purpose and meaning.

In this powerful book, Ryuho Okawa reveals the transcendent nature of consciousness and the secrets of our multidimensional universe and our place in it. By understanding the different stages of love and following the Buddhist Eightfold Path, he believes we can speed up our eternal process of development. *The Laws of the Sun* shows the way to realize true happiness—a happiness that continues from this world through the other.

For a complete list of books, visit **okawabooks.com**

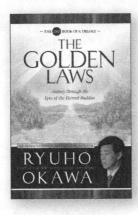

THE GOLDEN LAWS
HISTORY THROUGH THE EYES OF THE ETERNAL BUDDHA

Paperback • 201 pages • $14.95
ISBN: 978-1-941779-81-1

Throughout history, Great Guiding Spirits of Light have been present on Earth in both the East and the West at crucial points in human history to further our spiritual development. *The Golden Laws* reveals how Divine Plan has been unfolding on Earth, and outlines 5,000 years of the secret history of humankind. Once we understand the true course of history, through past, present and into the future, we cannot help but become aware of the significance of our spiritual mission in the present age.

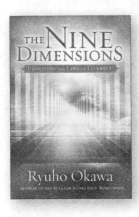

THE NINE DIMENSIONS
UNVEILING THE LAWS OF ETERNITY

Paperback • 168 pages • $15.95
ISBN: 978-0-982698-56-3

This book is a window into the mind of our loving God, who designed this world and the vast, wondrous world of our afterlife as a school with many levels through which our souls learn and grow. When the religions and cultures of the world discover the truth of their common spiritual origin, they will be inspired to accept their differences, come together under faith in God, and build an era of harmony and peaceful progress on Earth.

For a complete list of books, visit ***okawabooks.com***

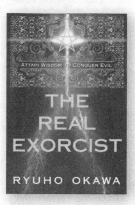

THE REAL EXORCIST
ATTAIN WISDOM TO CONQUER EVIL

Paperback • 208 pages • $16.95
ISBN:978-1-942125-67-9

This is a profound spiritual text backed by the author's nearly forty years of real-life experience with spiritual phenomena. In it, Okawa teaches how we may discern and overcome our negative tendencies, by acquiring the right knowledge, mindset and lifestyle.

THE NEW RESURRECTION
MY MIRACULOUS STORY OF OVERCOMING ILLNESS AND DEATH

Hardcover • 224 pages • $19.95
ISBN: 978-1-942125-64-8

The New Resurrection is an autobiographical account of an astonishing miracle experienced by author Ryuho Okawa in 2004. This event was adapted into the feature-length film *Immortal Hero*, released in Japan, the United States and Canada during the Fall of 2019. Today, Okawa lives each day with the readiness to die for the Truth and has dedicated his life to selflessly guide faith seekers towards spiritual development and happiness. In testament to Okawa's earnest resolve, the appendix showcases a myriad of accomplishments by Okawa, chronicled after his miraculous resurrection.

For a complete list of books, visit **okawabooks.com**

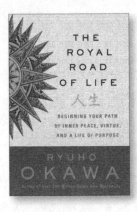

THE ROYAL ROAD OF LIFE

BEGINNING YOUR PATH OF INNER PEACE, VIRTUE, AND A LIFE OF PURPOSE

Paperback • 224 pages • $16.95
ISBN: 978-1-942125-53-2

With over 30 years of lectures and teachings spanning diverse topics of faith, self-growth, leadership (and more), Ryuho Okawa presents the profound eastern wisdom that he has cultivated on his approach to life. *The Royal Road of Life* illuminates a path to becoming a person of virtue, whose character and depth will move and inspire others towards the same meaningful destination.

THE STARTING POINT OF HAPPINESS

AN INSPIRING GUIDE TO POSITIVE LIVING WITH FAITH, LOVE, AND COURAGE

Paperback • 224 pages • $16.95
ISBN: 978-1-942125-26-6

In this book, Ryuho Okawa awakens us to the true spiritual values of our life; he beautifully illustrates, in simple but profound words, how we can find purpose and meaning in life and attain happiness that lasts forever. This self-renewing guide to positive living will awaken us to the spiritual truths, infuse us with hope, strength and fulfillment, and lead us to walk the path to authentic, lasting happiness.

---

*For a complete list of books, visit **okawabooks.com***

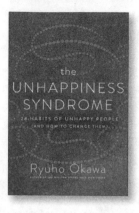

THE UNHAPPINESS SYNDROME

28 HABITS OF UNHAPPY PEOPLE (AND HOW TO CHANGE THEM)

Paperback • 192 pages • $15.95
ISBN: 978-1-942125-16-7

In this book, Ryuho Okawa diagnoses the 28 common habits of the Unhappiness Syndrome and offers prescriptions for changing them so that we can cure ourselves of this syndrome. Find out whether you fall into any of the 28 patterns so that you can free yourself from worries, distress, and emotional pain. With the prescriptions offered in this book, you can start to think and act in a way that attracts happiness and open a path to a positive, bright, and happy future!

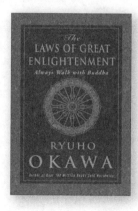

THE LAWS OF GREAT ENLIGHTENMENT

ALWAYS WALK WITH BUDDHA

Paperback • 232 pages • $17.95
ISBN: 978-1-942125-62-4

Constant self-blame for mistakes, setbacks, or failures and feelings of unforgivingness toward others are hard to overcome. Through the power of enlightenment we can learn to forgive ourselves and others, overcome life's problems, and courageously create a brighter future ourselves. *The Laws of Great Enlightenment* addresses the core problems of life that people often struggle with and offers advice on how to overcome them based on spiritual truths.

---

*For a complete list of books, visit **okawabooks.com***

THE LAWS OF SUCCESS
A SPIRITUAL GUIDE TO TURNING YOUR HOPES INTO REALITY

Paperback • 208 pages • $15.95
ISBN: 978-1-942125-15-0

The Laws of Success offers 8 spiritual principles that, when put to practice in our day-to-day life, will help us attain lasting success and let us experience the fulfillment of living our purpose and the joy of sharing our happiness with many others. The timeless wisdom and practical steps that Ryuho Okawa offers will guide us through any difficulties and problems we may face in life, and serve as guiding principles for living a positive, constructive, and meaningful life.

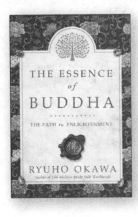

THE ESSENCE OF BUDDHA
THE PATH TO ENLIGHTENMENT

Paperback • 208 pages • $14.95
ISBN: 978-1-942125-06-8

In this book, Ryuho Okawa imparts in simple and accessible language his wisdom about the essence of Shakyamuni Buddha's philosophy of life and enlightenment–teachings that have been inspiring people all over the world for over 2,500 years. By offering a new perspective on core Buddhist thoughts that have long been cloaked in mystique, Okawa brings these teachings to life for modern people. *The Essence of Buddha* distills a way of life that anyone can practice to achieve a life of self-growth, compassionate living, and true happiness.

For a complete list of books, visit **okawabooks.com**

LOVE FOR THE FUTURE
Building One World of Freedom and Democracy Under God's Truth

THE HELL YOU NEVER KNEW
And How to Avoid Going There

WORRY-FREE LIVING
Let Go of Stress and Live in Peace and Happiness

THE STRONG MIND
The Art of Building the Inner Strength
to Overcome Life's Difficulties

HEALING FROM WITHIN
Life-Changing Keys to Calm, Spiritual, and Healthy Living

THINK BIG!
Be Positive and Be Brave to Achieve Your Dreams

THE MIRACLE OF MEDITATION
Opening Your Life to Peace, Joy, and the Power Within

THE HEART OF WORK
10 Keys to Living Your Calling

INVITATION TO HAPPINESS
7 Inspirations from Your Inner Angel

For a complete list of books, visit **okawabooks.com**